Every Minute of the Day with the Lord Journal

GEORGE W. BAUM

authorHOUSE®

AuthorHouse™
1663 Liberty Drive
Bloomington, IN 47403
www.authorhouse.com
Phone: 1 (800) 839-8640

Published by AuthorHouse   06/19/2017

ISBN: 978-1-5246-9668-9 (sc)
ISBN: 978-1-5246-9666-5 (hc)
ISBN: 978-1-5246-9667-2 (e)

Library of Congress Control Number: 2017909349

Print information available on the last page.

KJV – King James Version
Scripture taken from the King James Version of the Bible.

Interior Image Credit: Selket

This book is printed on acid-free paper.

This Journal
Belongs To

_____

This Journal is dedicated to my wonderful wife, Sue. Without her encouragement, support, and technical knowledge this work would not have been completed.

May the words of the LORD give you knowledge and strength.

May the words of the LORD give you comfort and peace.

May the words of the LORD give you guidance and salvation.

May you study, read, and be reminded of what
the LORD has to say to you today,

so that the truth and love found in HIS word
will be with you every minute of the day.

Amen

EVERY MINUTE OF THE DAY WITH THE LORD

One day, very early in the morning, I was unable to go back to sleep because I was thinking about a project I was working on. I decided to look at the clock to see what time it was and the clock said 3:16. I immediately thought of John 3:16. That started me thinking about another project. How about time reminding me of different Bible verses in the Bible.

HOW IT WORKS

Using the 24 hour clock system, like the military does, plan to have a scripture verse cover every minute of the day. Any time between 1300 and 1313 could remind you of the entire chapter of 1 Corinthians 13. 0610 thru 0617 might remind you of Ephesians 6:10-17, "The Armor of God". Be creative. For instance 0**91**0 could be given to Psalm 91. Remember each verse gets a minute. So if you like all of Psalm 91, the time slot between 0**91**0 and 0916 would be used. Some scriptures, of course, could be challenging. The familiar Psalm 27:1 for example. "The Lord is my light and my salvation; whom shall I fear? the Lord is the strength of my life; of whom shall I be afraid"? (KJV) There is no time slot that fits that scripture. At the same time, there is no scripture in the Bible that can fill in 23:58 (the time on the cover). You may want to assign scriptures that have no corresponding time slots to time slots that have no corresponding scriptures.

HOW IT'S DONE

Get a sheet of paper. Start by putting your favorite scriptures in the time slots that would be the closest to the location of those scriptures in the Bible and record them on the paper. If some of your favorite scriptures have similar locations, put your most favorite in the time slot. You could use the same time slot for both scriptures or choose another slot. If you cannot find a time slot that works for a scripture's location because of its numbers be creative. Once you have given all of your favorite scriptures a time slot, find some new ones to fill in some more slots. Don't forget the early morning time slots. You may find yourself unable to go back to sleep and the scriptures the clock is reminding you of may help to calm your sprit. It may not be a bad idea to assign soothing scriptures to those time slots. Over time you may have your whole day filled with scripture.

It may take some time to get all of the slots filled but it will be worth it. There are 1440 minutes in a day. That means you have the potential of memorizing almost as many verses found in Matthew (1070) and 1 Corinthians (437) combined (1507).

Now, if trying to memorize 1440 verses seems rather intimidating, use the time to remind yourself of some of your favorite parables. For example, 1030 to 1037 could remind you of Luke 10:30-37, the parable of the Good Samaritan. Oh by the way, if 1030 to 1037 is taken you could use 2234-2240 or 1228-1231 (Matthew 22:34-40, Mark 12:28-31). They also contain the same parable.

If you want to remember prophecies, 0501-0504 could remind you of Micah 5:1-4, the prophecy of the birth of Jesus. If you are interested in history, 1701-1754 could be used for 1 Samuel 17:1-54, the story of David and Goliath.

HAVE FUN

So the next time you look at your watch or cell phone for the time and after you say "Oh I'm late!", think of the corresponding scripture that is related to that time slot and repeat it. You know you will be checking the time often while waiting in a doctor's office. What a good time to practice saying the corresponding scriptures or remembering the story associated with that time slot. And when you are unable to go back to sleep and you check the clock to see just how dadgum early it is, try repeating the scripture in that time slot.

Mix and match the minutes of the day with scripture. Remember, the Lord spends 1440 minutes a day with you. Now is your chance to spend 1440 minutes a day with the Lord.

I hope you enjoy spending every minute of the day with the Lord. May God bless you in all that you do. GWB

HOW TO USE YOUR TIME

What you just finished reading was a pamphlet I wrote earlier this year with the same title of this journal. I refer to it as a journal because it will become a record of how you spend every minute of the day with the Lord. After I wrote the pamphlet, I discovered that I had no place to write down the passages and verses in an organized way. I also discovered two additional things. First, there are passages that do not have a time period that will work such as Psalm 91. And second, you can spend every minute of the day with the Lord without having a verse in a time slot.

As the result of these discoveries I decided to publish this time journal that you might consider using, not only to record your Bible verses, but also the other times you spend with the Lord. For example, you may have a certain time of the day you do your personal Bible study and devotion. Put that in the time period provided in this journal. Your prayer time can also be put in the appropriate time period. You also may have a time reserved for your family to be together like at dinner. Put that in a time period. You don't need to be exact, just put the approximate time period.

Another use for this journal could be to record other wonderful moments in your life. For example, most parents are aware of the hour and minute their children are born. Put the child's name and date of their birth by the appropriate time. You may want to put your grandchild's date of birth by the appropriate time. For the time of your wedding, put "Wedding" and the year in that time period. You don't have to put the day on any special moment just the time and date so it can remind you of the blessings the Lord has provided you.

This is your journal. It is not a diary. It is to help keep the Lord in focus as you go through your day. There will be bad days and good days. We all know that. This journal is for those good TIMES. To make you aware of all the Lord does provide for you. When you are down read your Bible to be uplifted and you might want to refer to your journal also.

There is something else you may want to consider. When you go to be with the Lord, this journal cannot go with you so one of your relatives may end up with it. What a wonderful keepsake this is for them. They can show their children what Bible verses you liked and what events in your life you held dear. In short, it tells them how you spent every minute of the day with the Lord. It may also give them the idea to start their own journal.

So the next time you are waiting for a flight early in the morning, or at the DMV or VA waiting to be served, understand you WILL look at the time. Let it remind you of a Bible verse or a special event or moment in your life. It will have a calming effect and it will remind you that the Lord IS with you every minute of the day.

Two final thoughts: First, I was asked about how long I thought a person might take to fill up this journal. I answered by saying "It is one day in a person's life that will take a lifetime to complete." Second, when you reach that point in life where you are no longer able to maintain your journal, you may want to ask the person who has your journal to make one last entry for you. That entry would be the time you went to be with the Lord.

May you be blessed spending every minute of the day with the Lord.

MY MINUTES WITH THE LORD

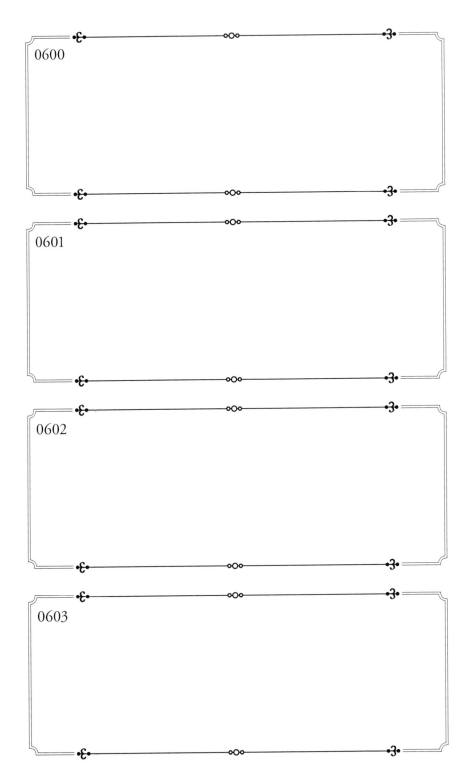

0600

0601

0602

0603

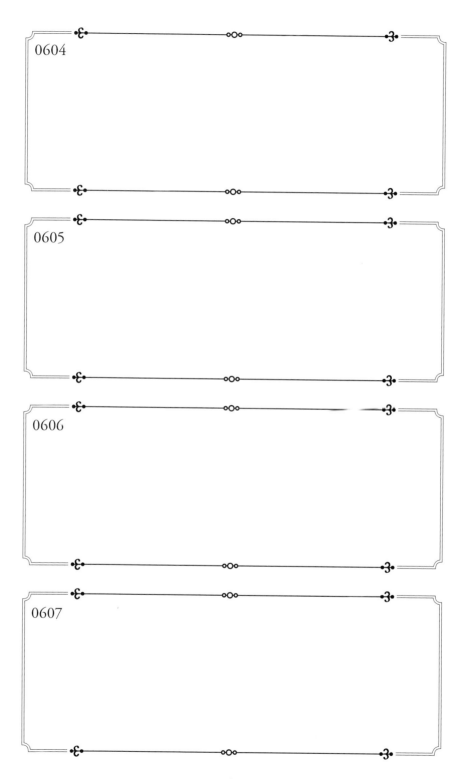

0604

0605

0606

0607

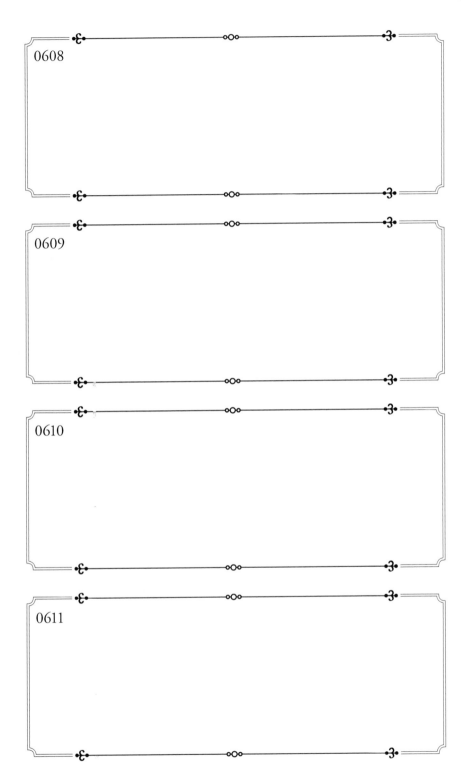

0608

0609

0610

0611

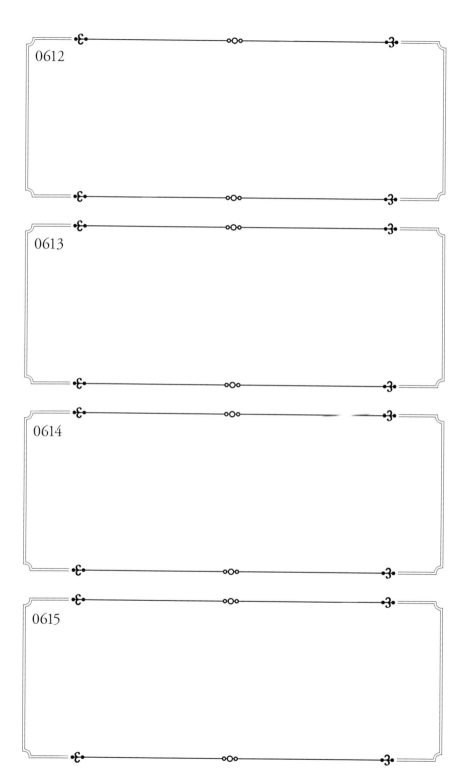

0612

0613

0614

0615

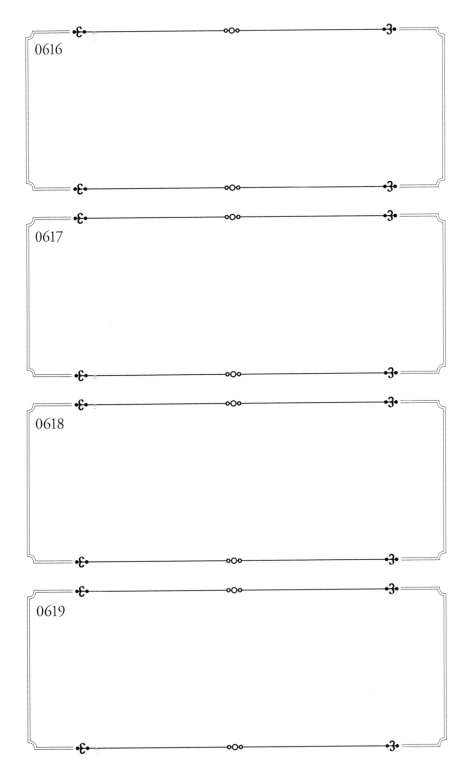

0616

0617

0618

0619

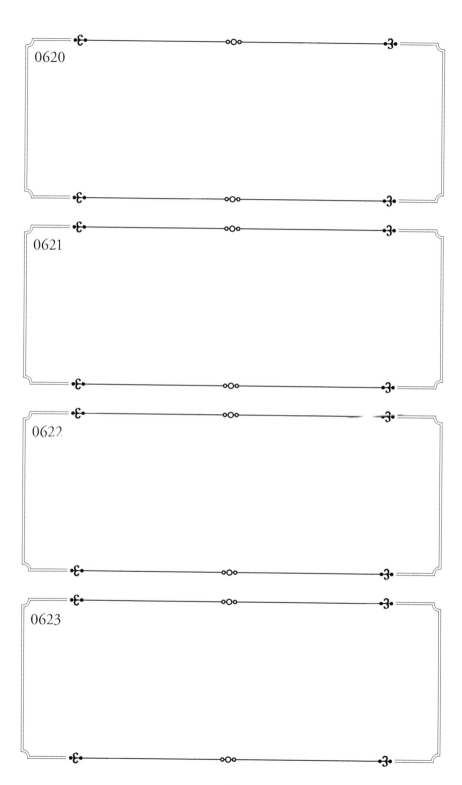

0620

0621

0622

0623

13

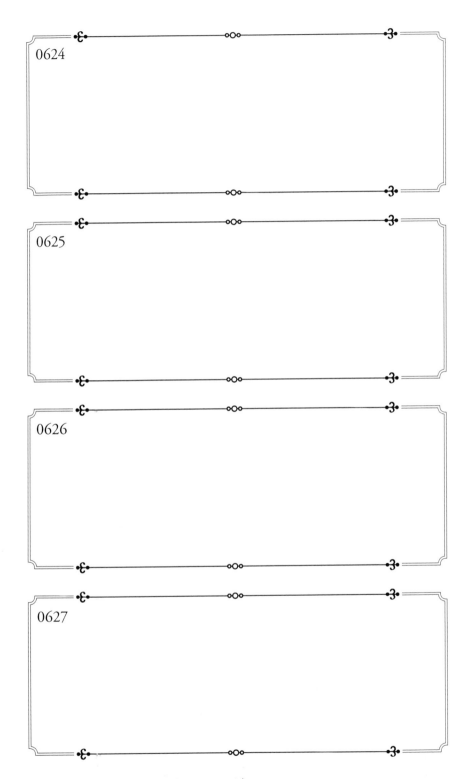

0624

0625

0626

0627

0628

0629

0630

0631

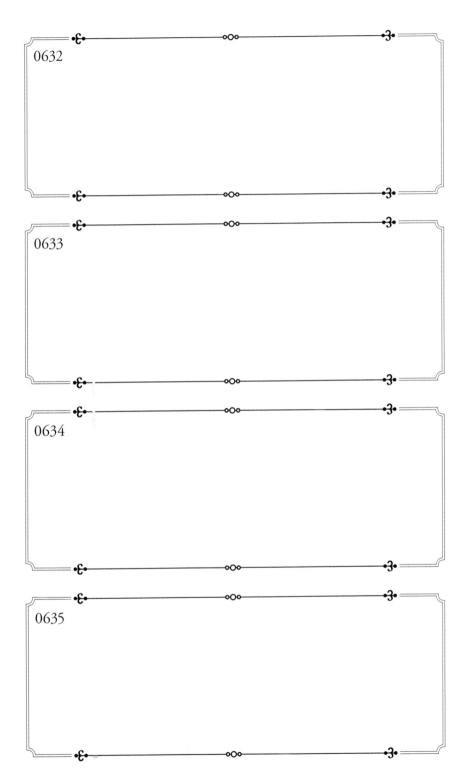

0632

0633

0634

0635

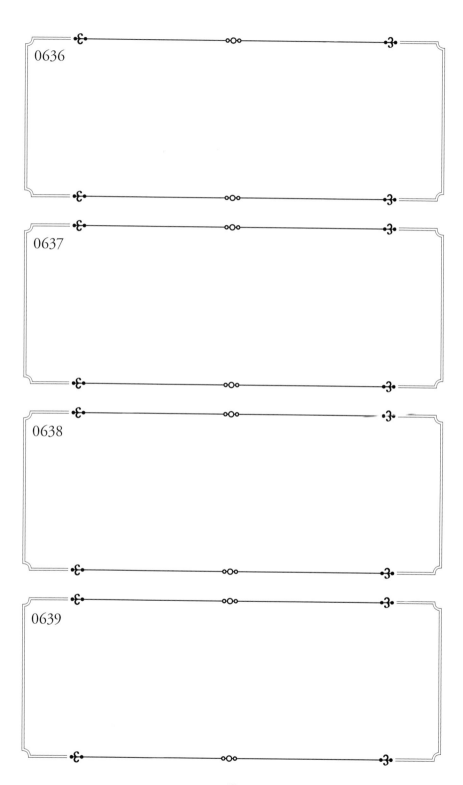

0636

0637

0638

0639

17

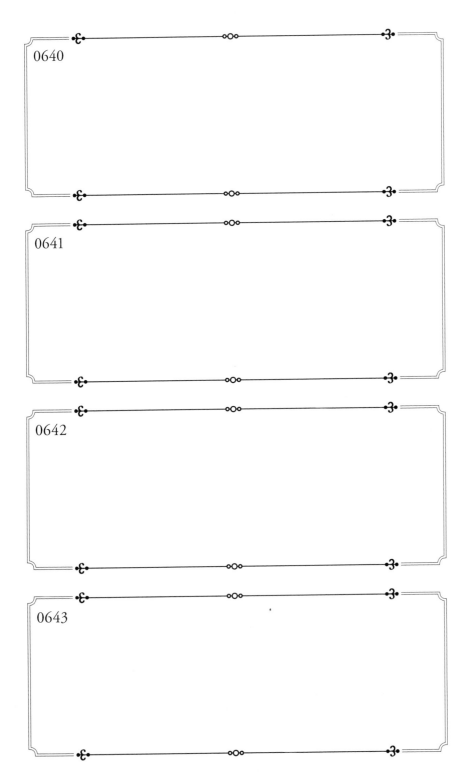

0640

0641

0642

0643

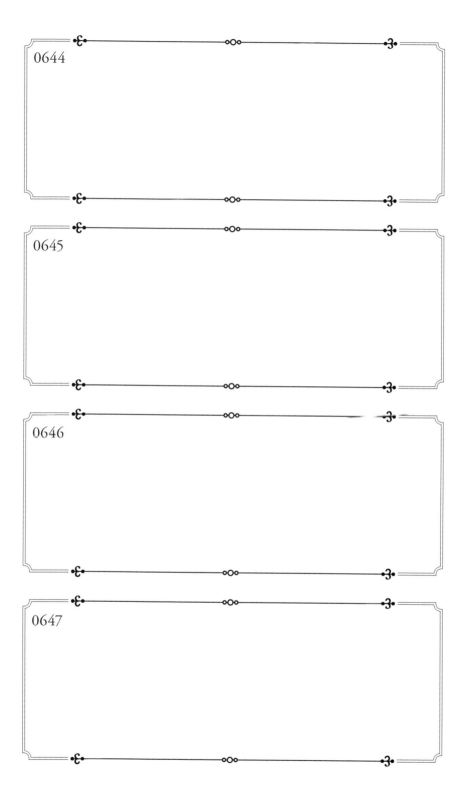

0644

0645

0646

0647

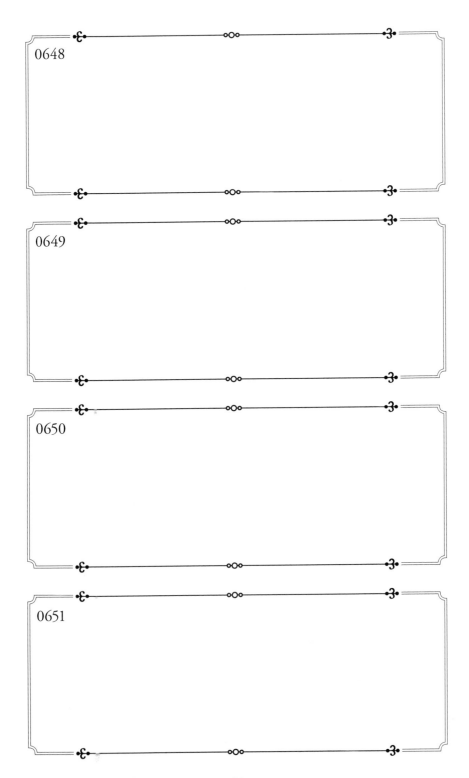

0648

0649

0650

0651

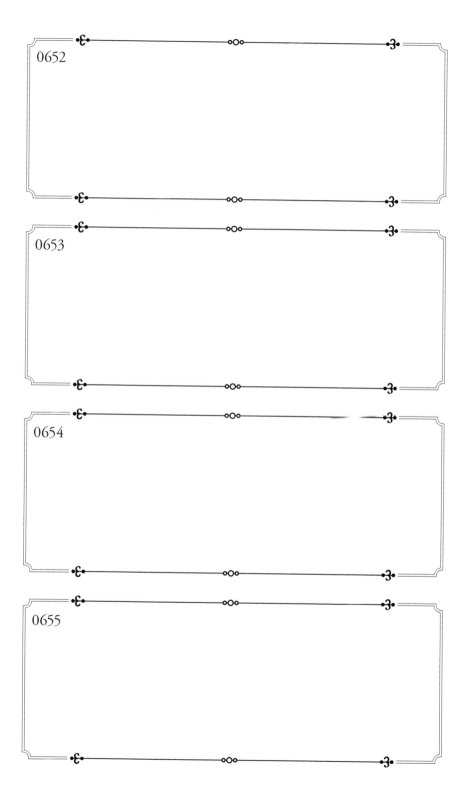

0652

0653

0654

0655

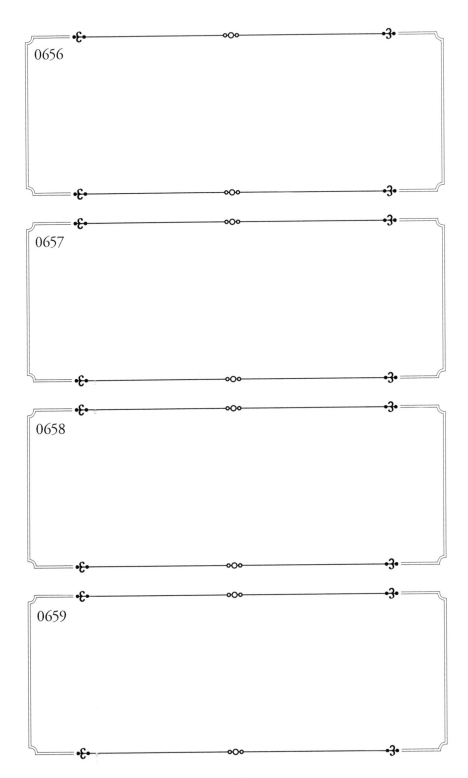

0656

0657

0658

0659

0700

0701

0702

0703

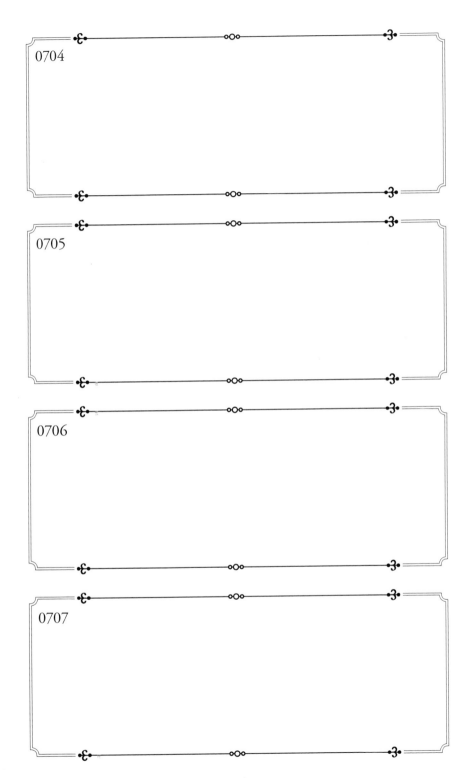

0704

0705

0706

0707

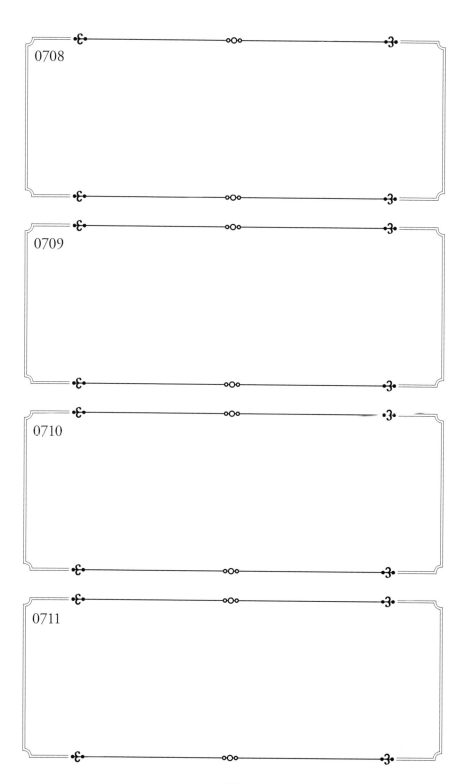

0708

0709

0710

0711

25

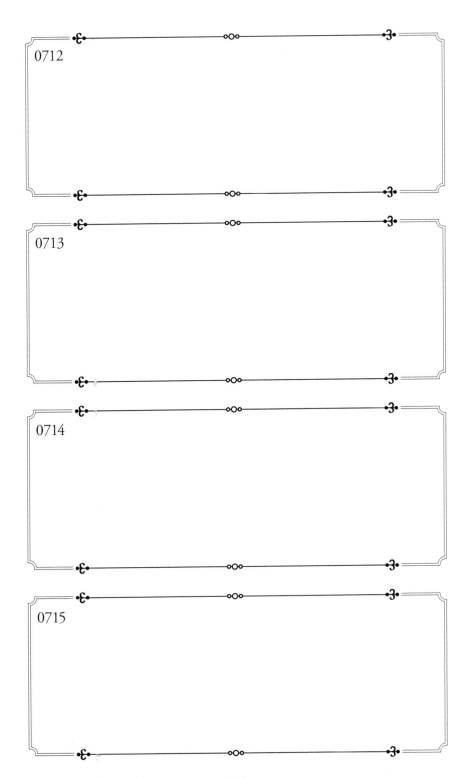

0712

0713

0714

0715

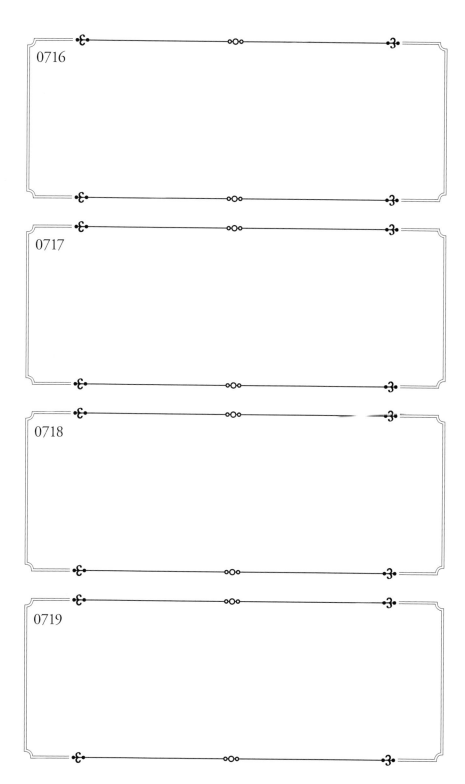

0716

0717

0718

0719

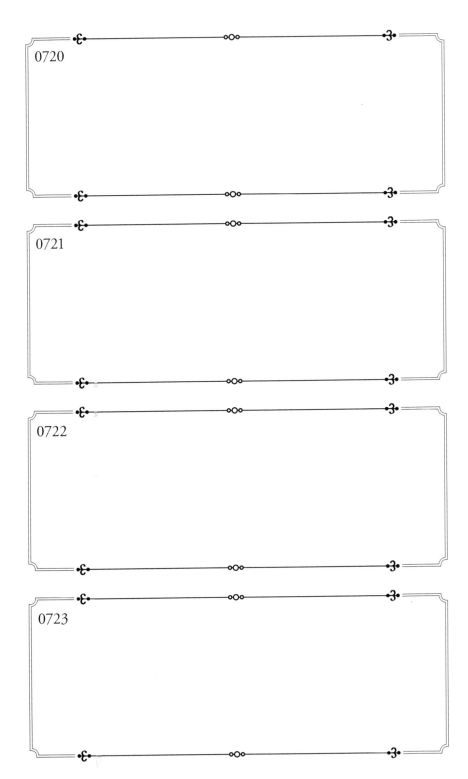

0720

0721

0722

0723

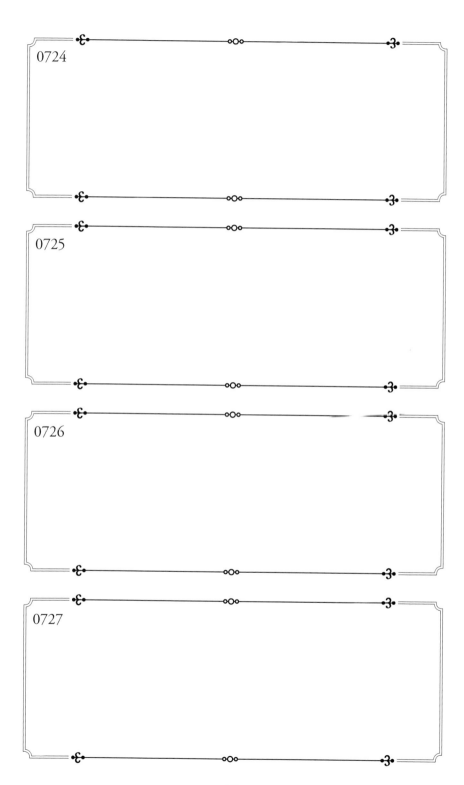

0724

0725

0726

0727

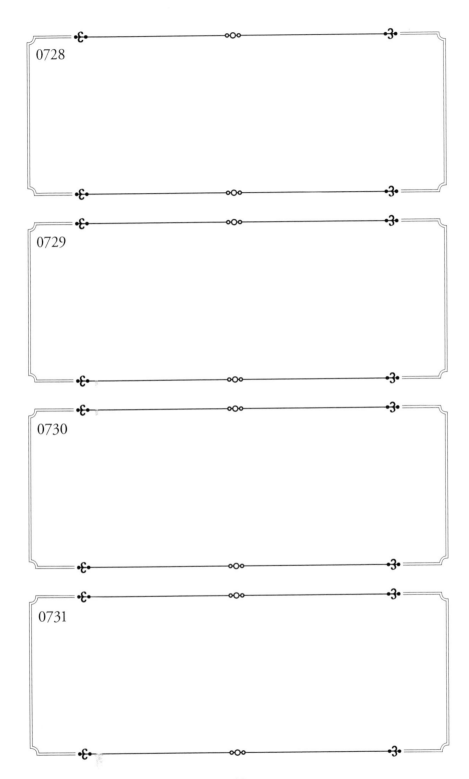

0728

0729

0730

0731

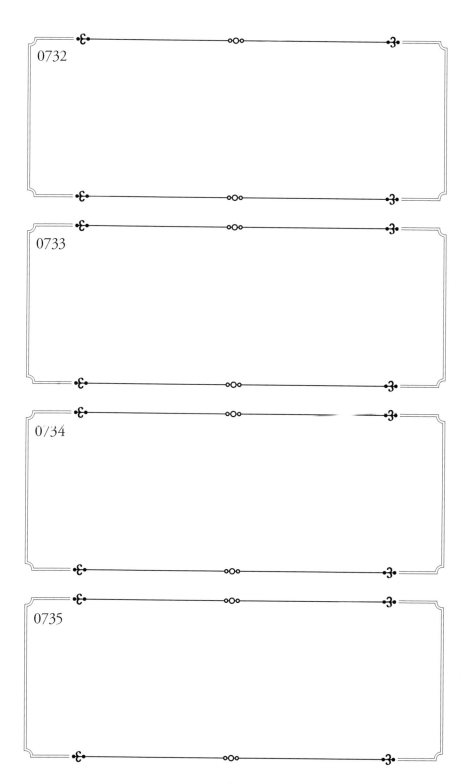

0732

0733

0/34

0735

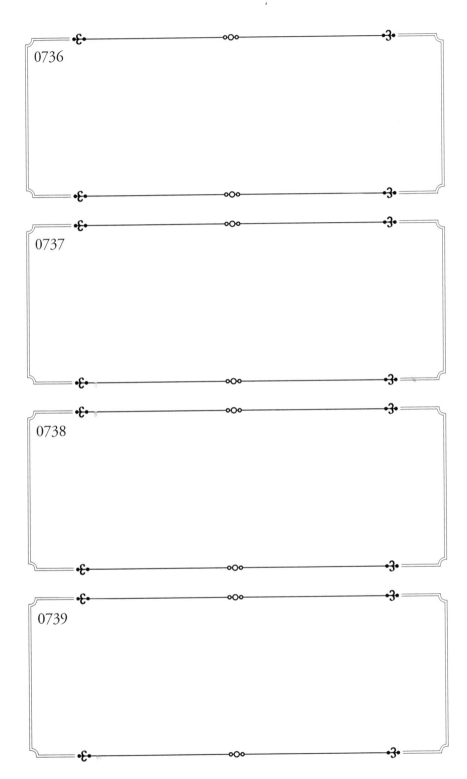

0736

0737

0738

0739

0740

0741

0742

0743

0744

0745

0746

0747

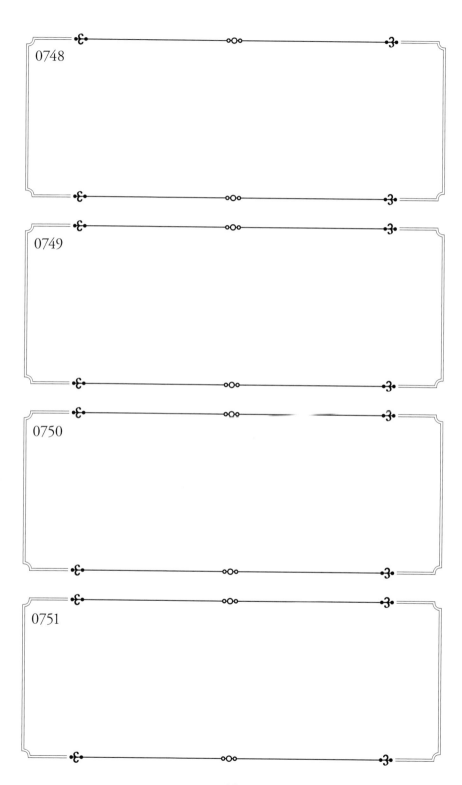

0748

0749

0750

0751

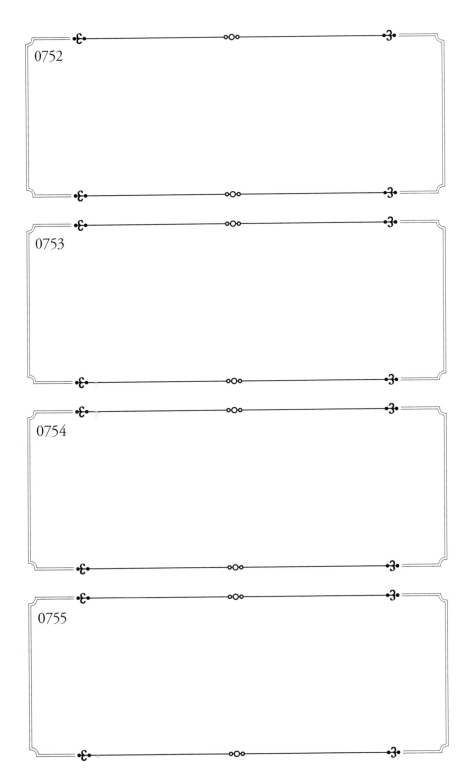

0752

0753

0754

0755

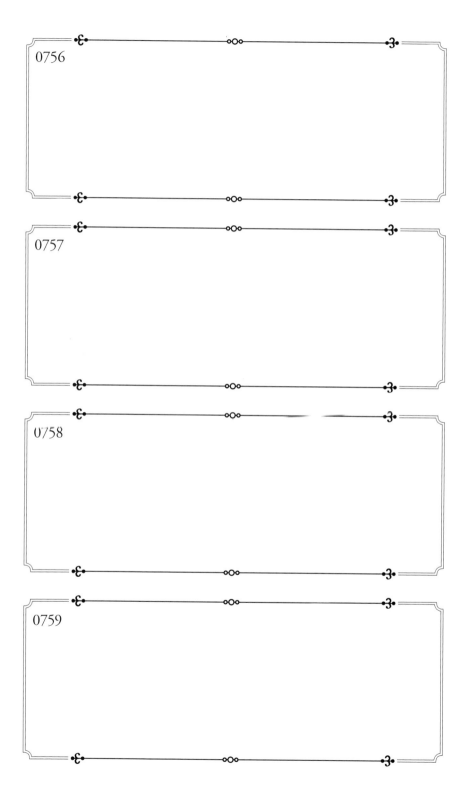

0756

0757

0758

0759

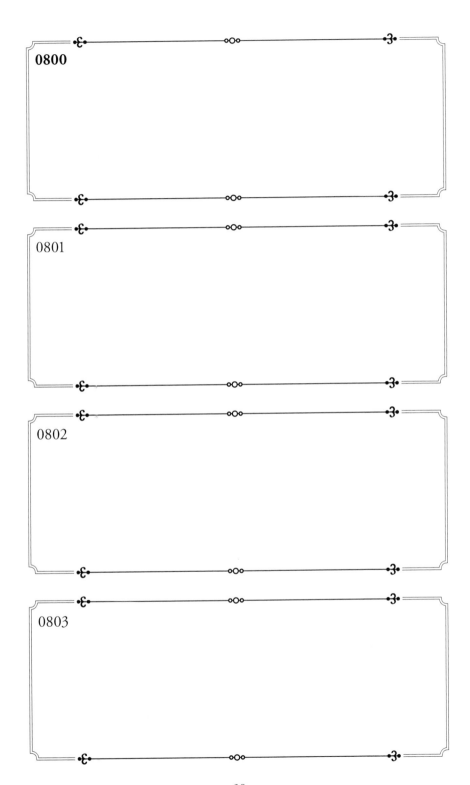

0800

0801

0802

0803

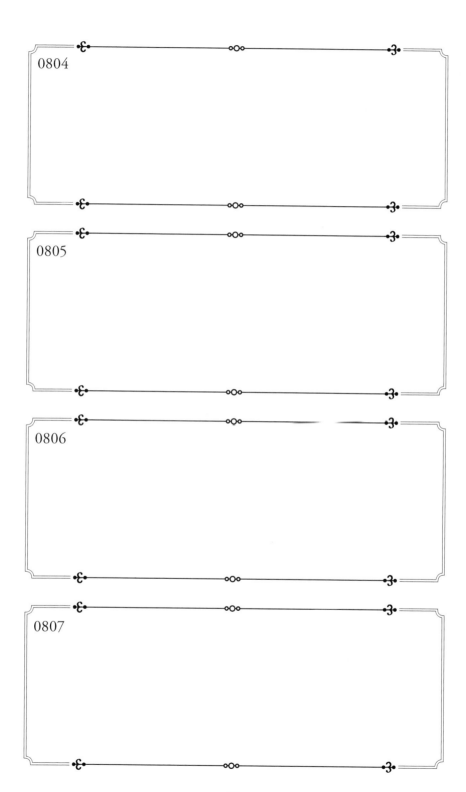

0804

0805

0806

0807

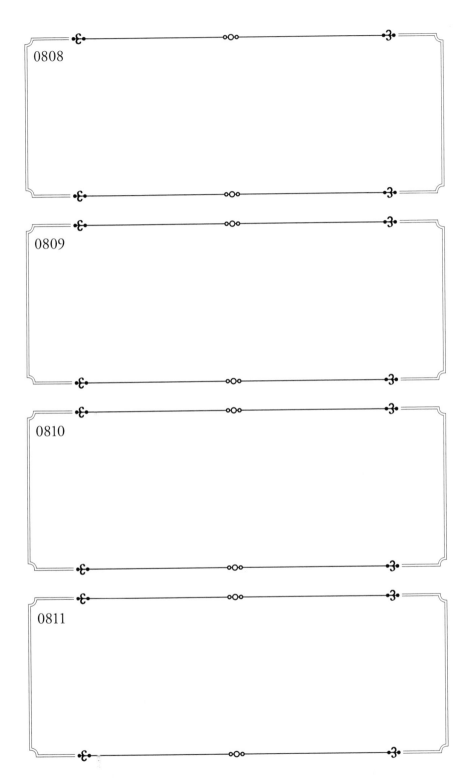

0808

0809

0810

0811

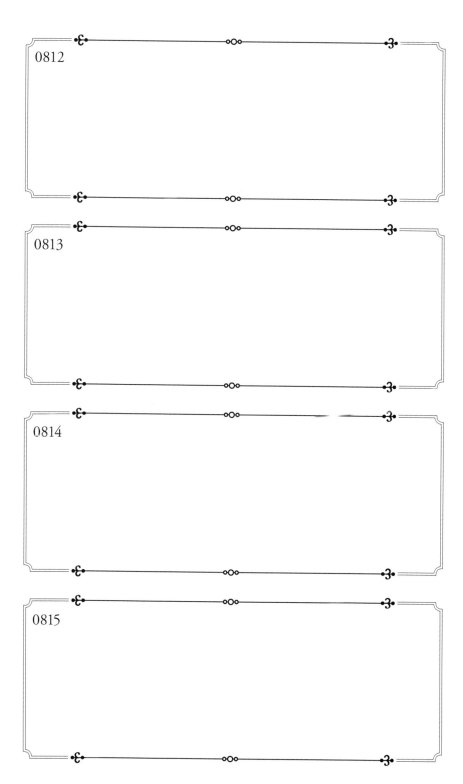

0812

0813

0814

0815

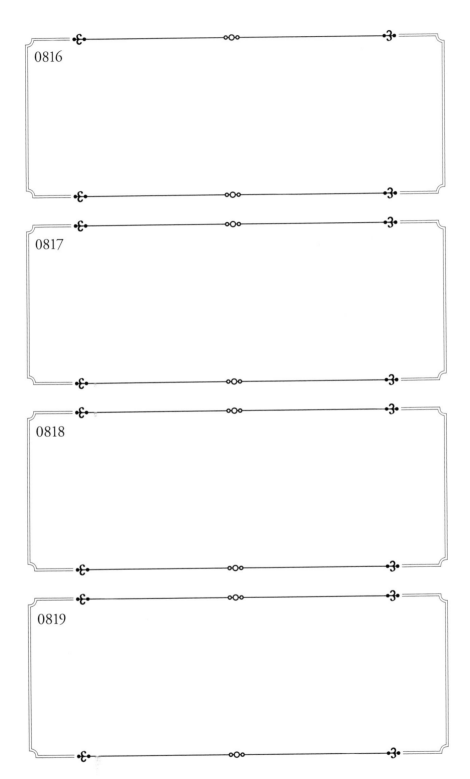

0816

0817

0818

0819

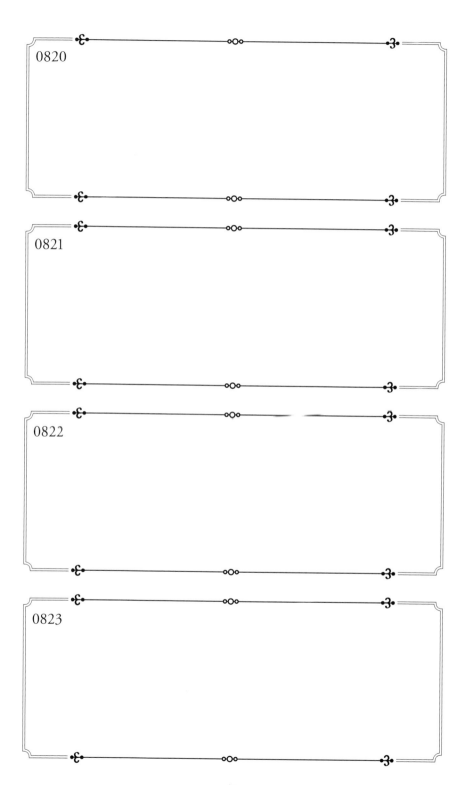

0820

0821

0822

0823

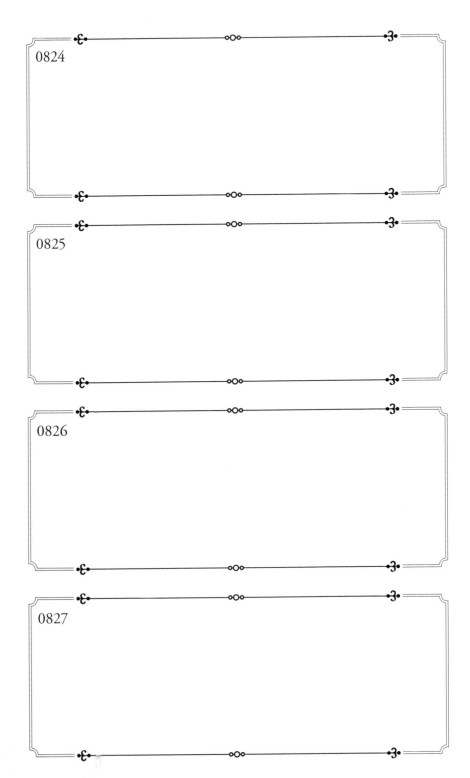

0824

0825

0826

0827

0828

0829

0830

0831

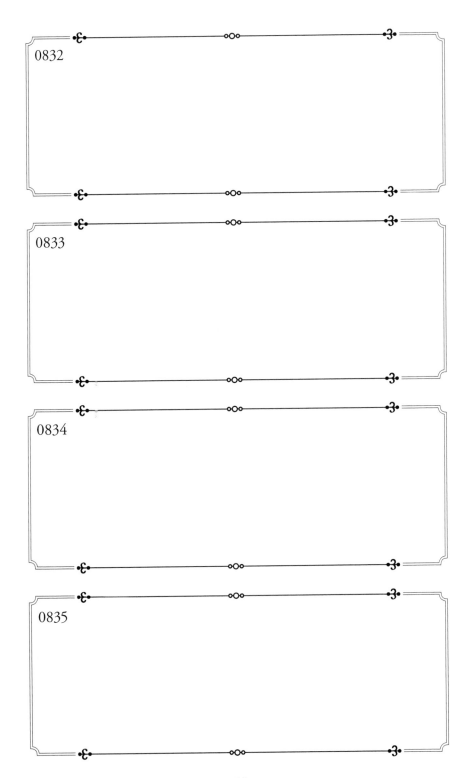

0832

0833

0834

0835

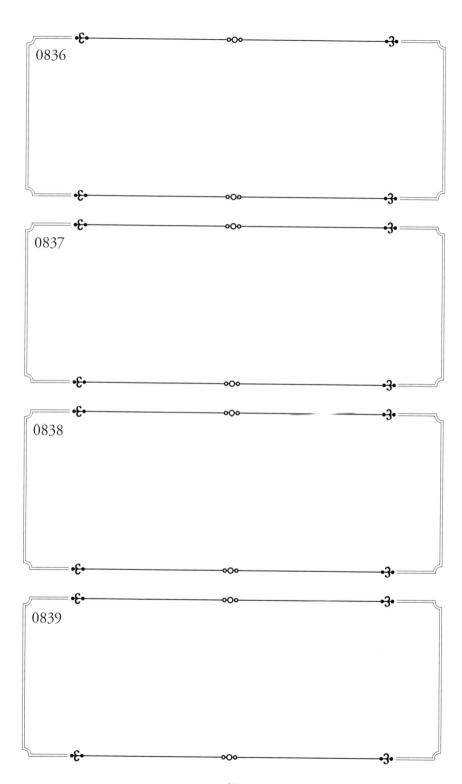

0836

0837

0838

0839

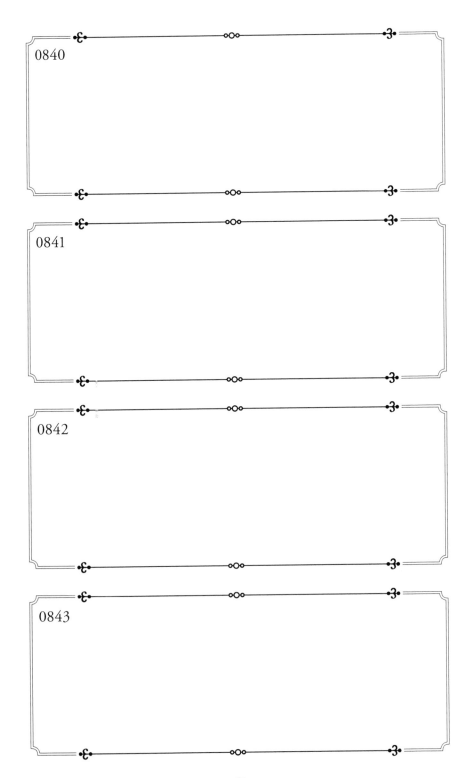

0840

0841

0842

0843

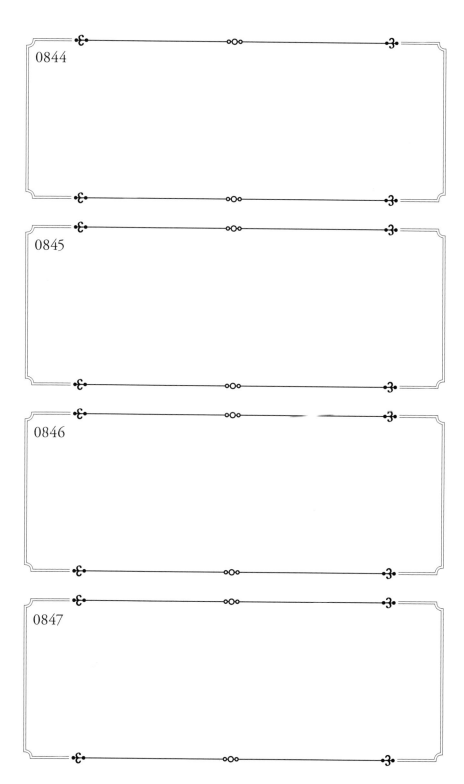

0844

0845

0846

0847

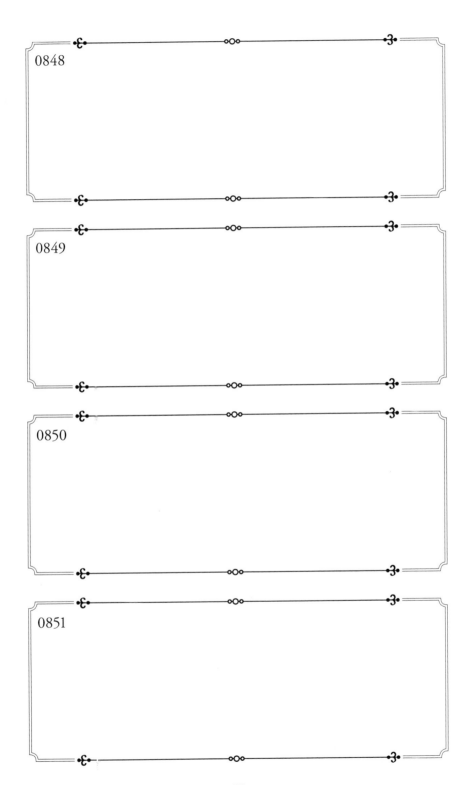

0848

0849

0850

0851

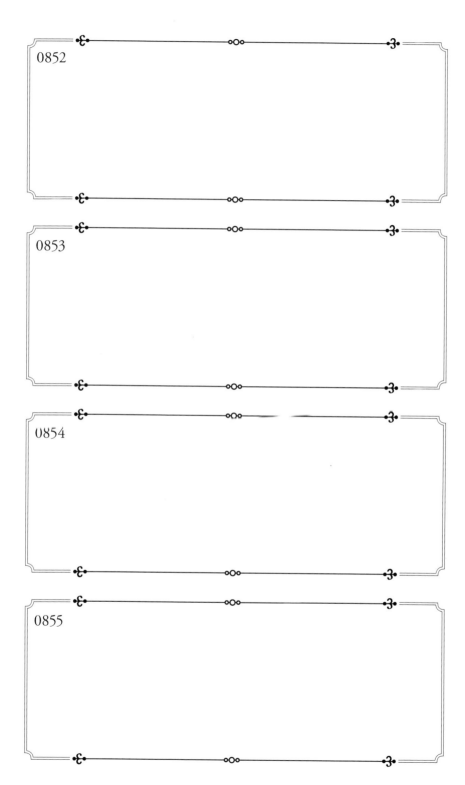

0852

0853

0854

0855

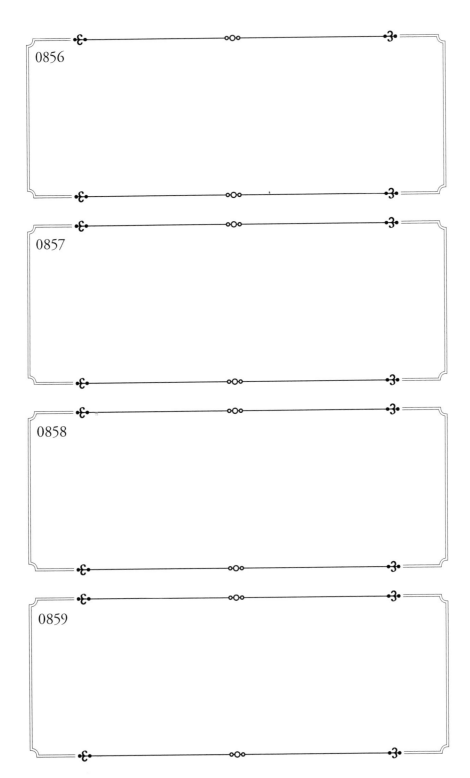

0856

0857

0858

0859

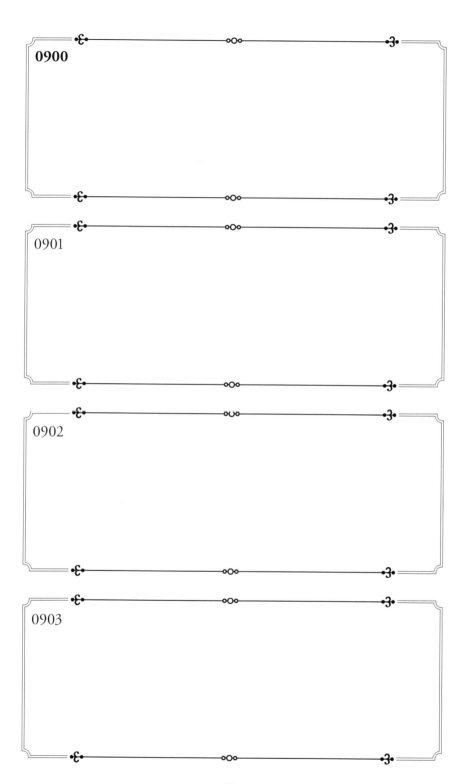

0900

0901

0902

0903

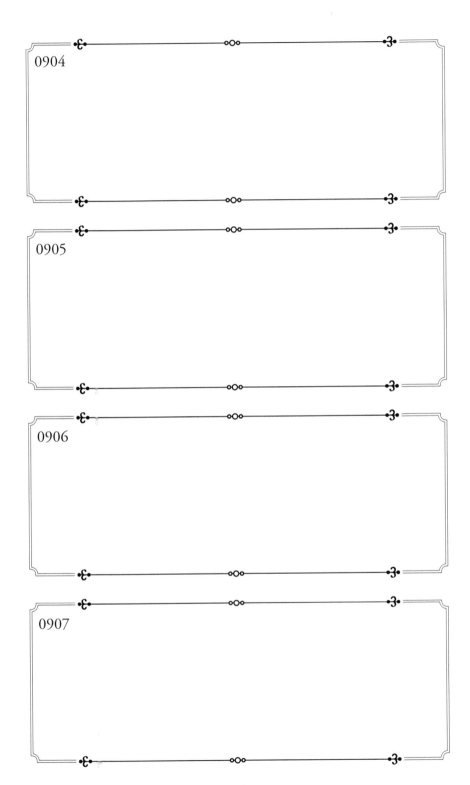

0904

0905

0906

0907

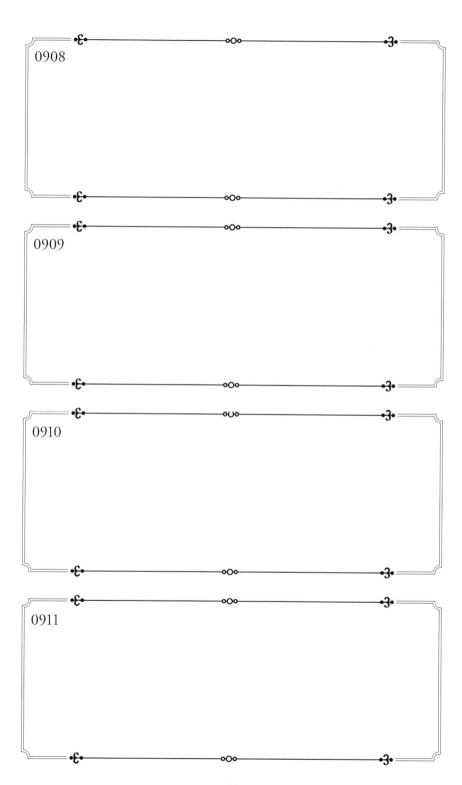

0908

0909

0910

0911

55

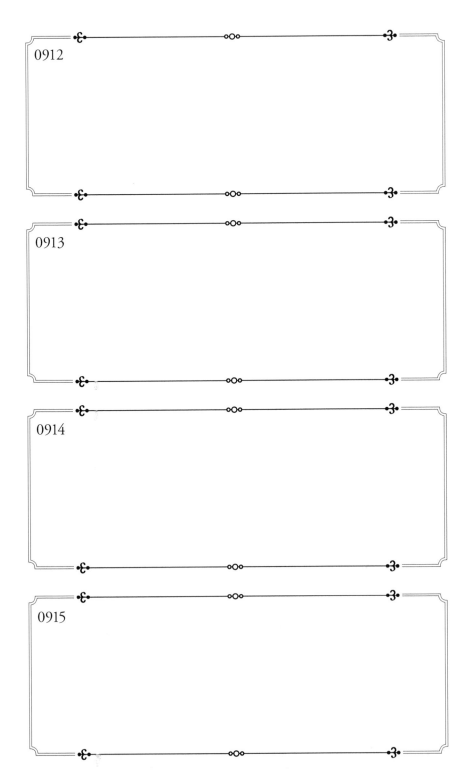

0912

0913

0914

0915

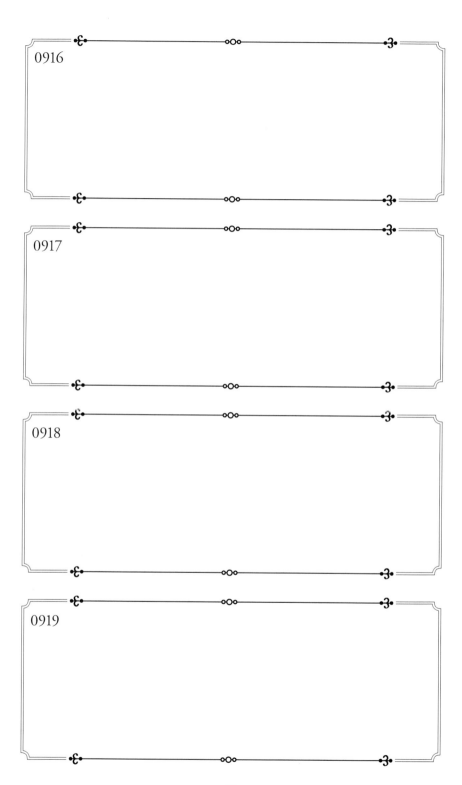

0916

0917

0918

0919

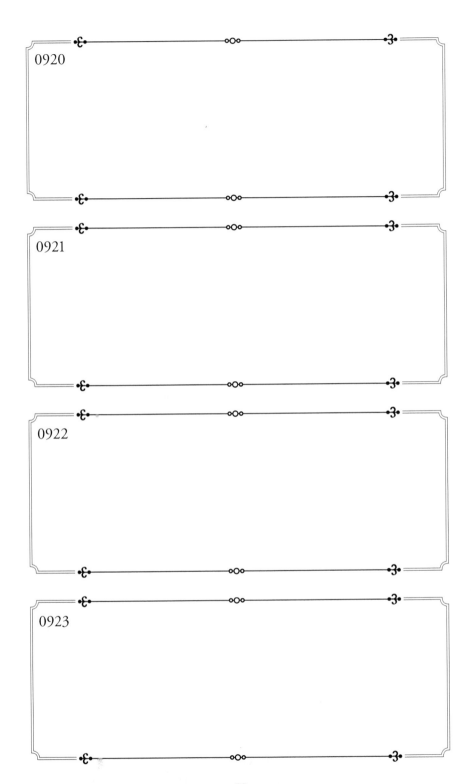

0920

0921

0922

0923

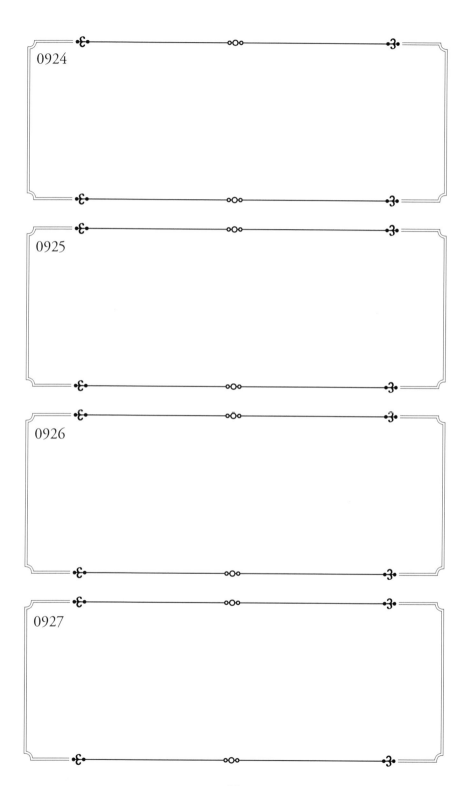

0924

0925

0926

0927

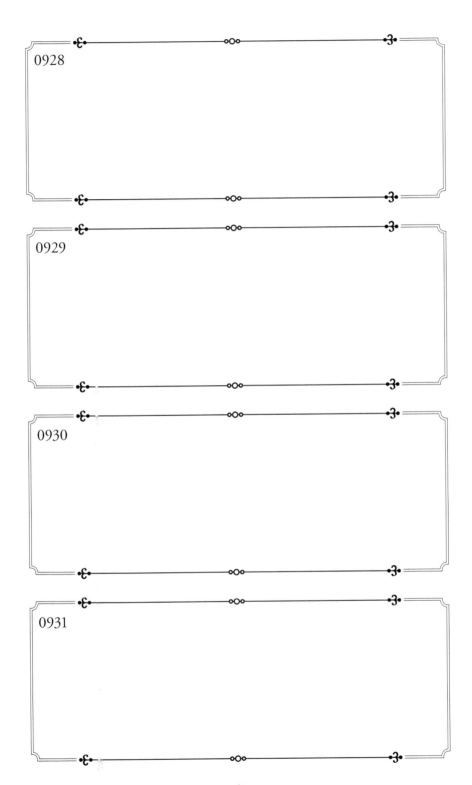

0928

0929

0930

0931

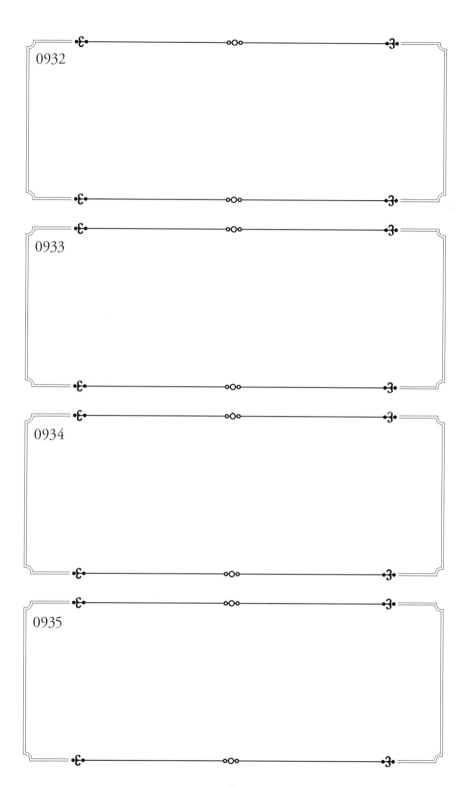

0932

0933

0934

0935

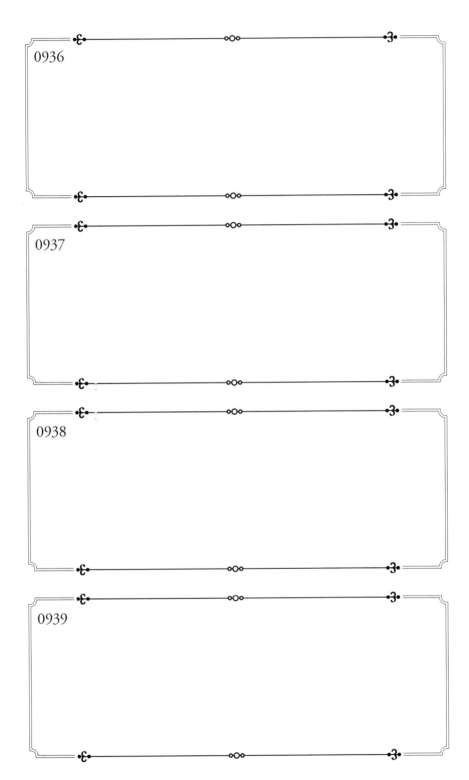

0936

0937

0938

0939

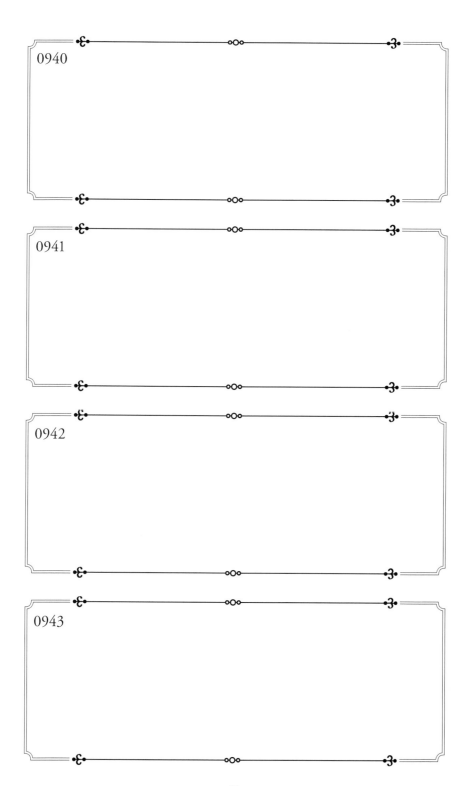

0940

0941

0942

0943

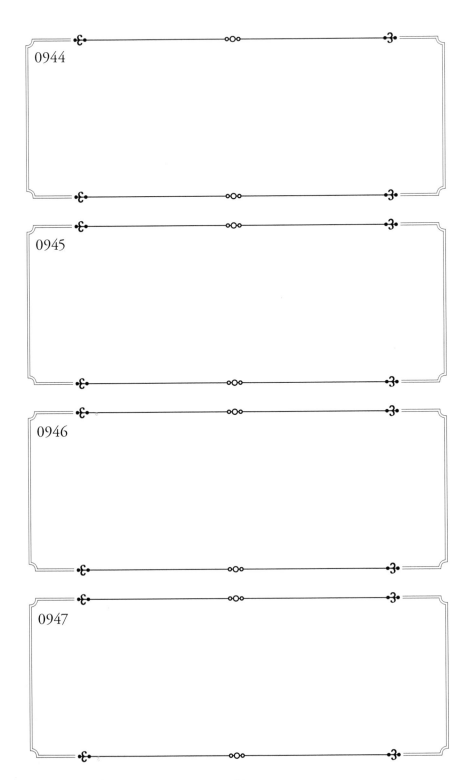

0944

0945

0946

0947

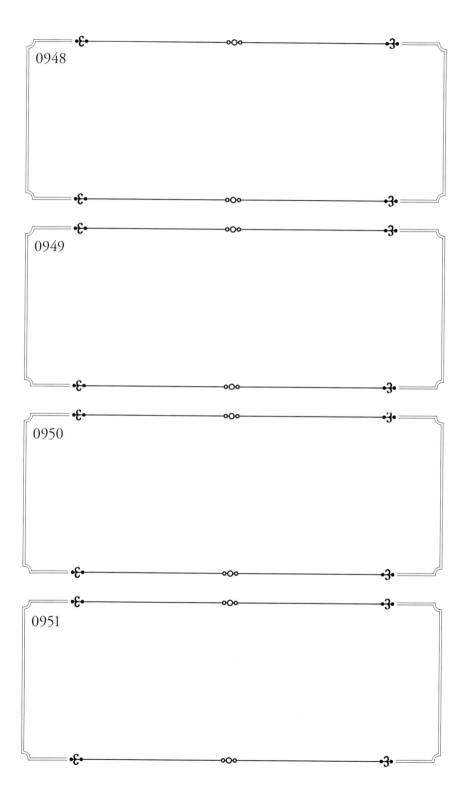

0948

0949

0950

0951

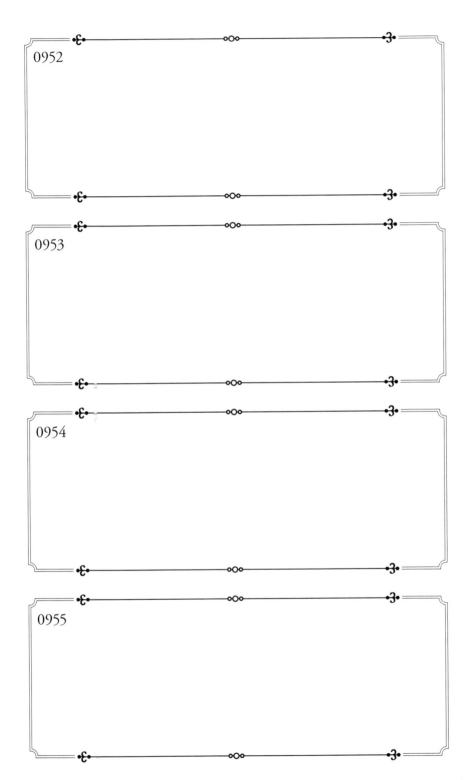

0952

0953

0954

0955

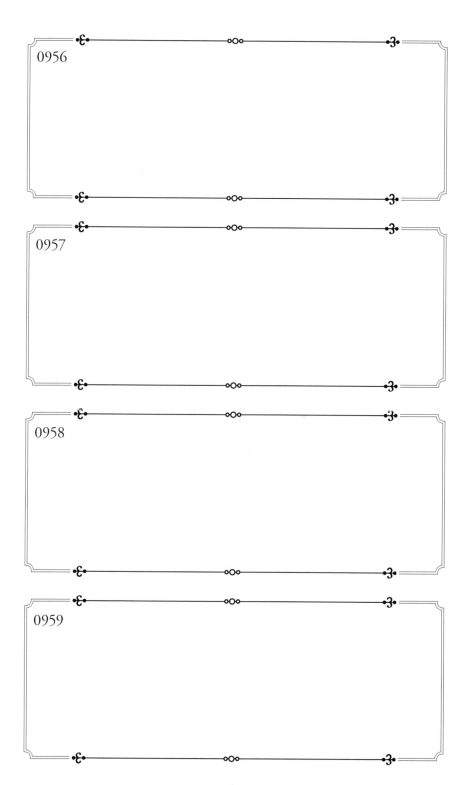

0956

0957

0958

0959

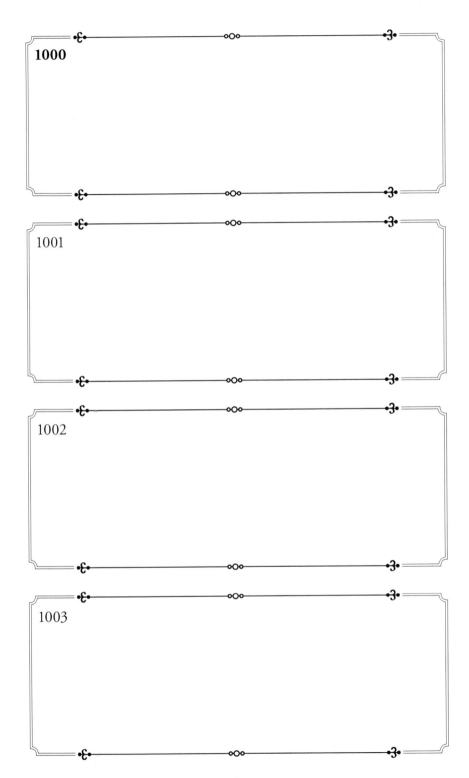

1000

1001

1002

1003

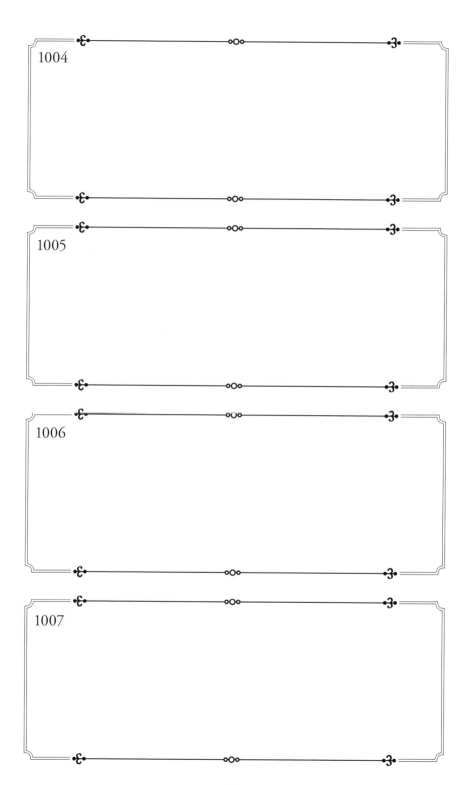

1004

1005

1006

1007

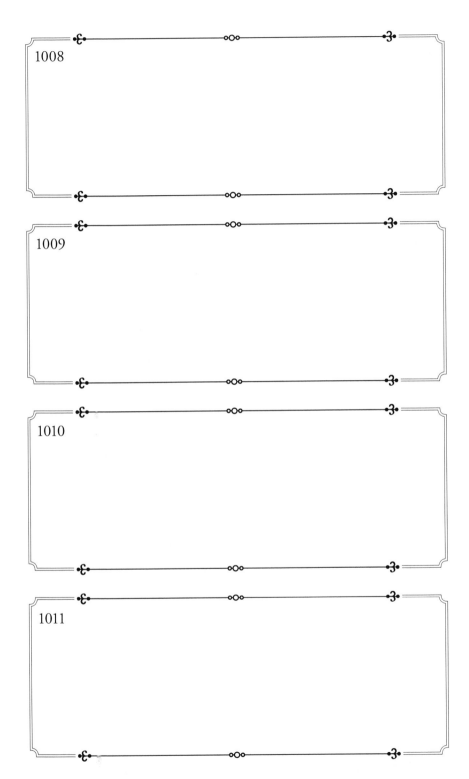

1008

1009

1010

1011

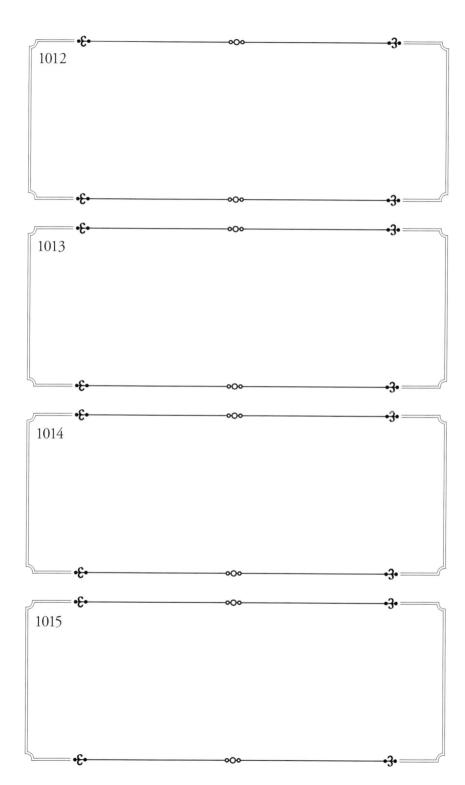

1012

1013

1014

1015

1016

1017

1018

1019

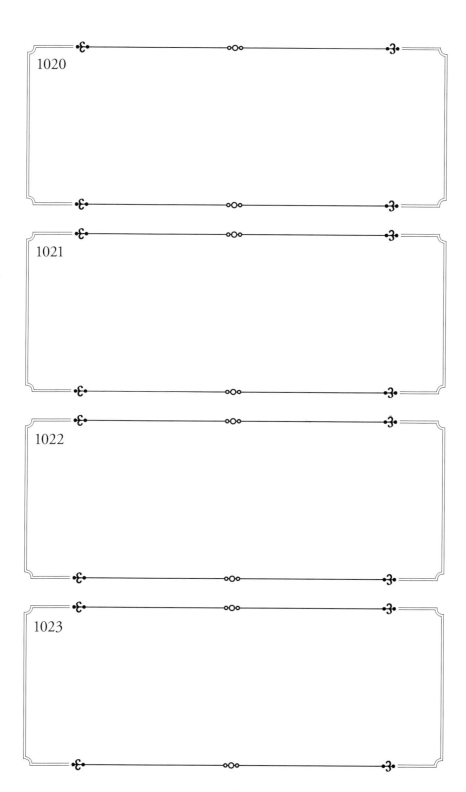

1020

1021

1022

1023

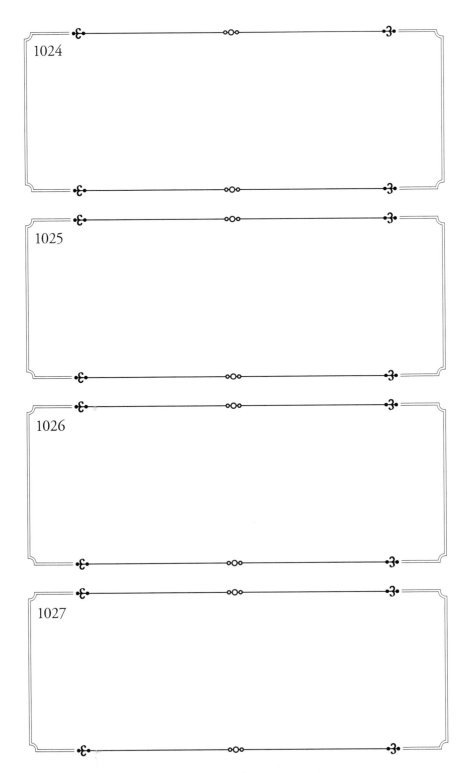

1024

1025

1026

1027

1028

1029

1030

1031

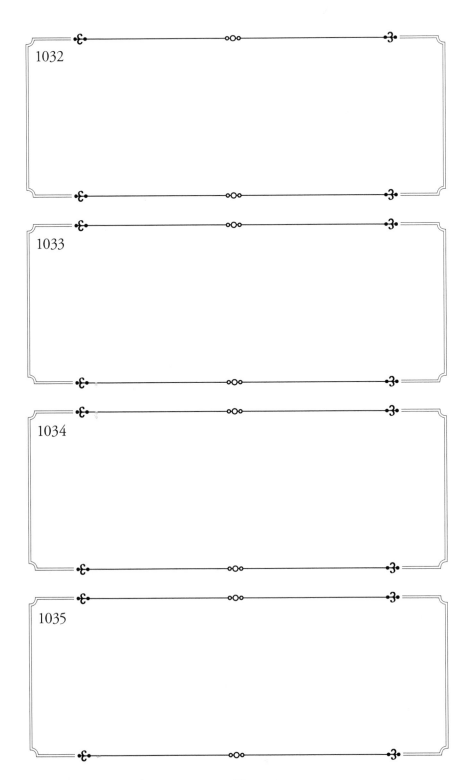

1032

1033

1034

1035

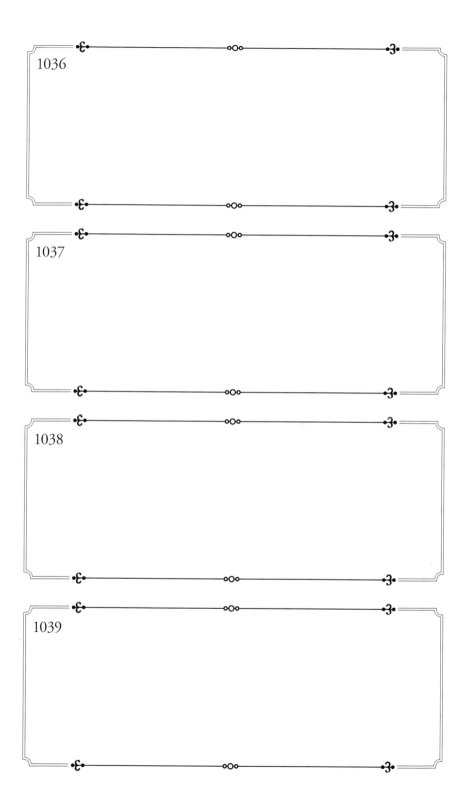

1036

1037

1038

1039

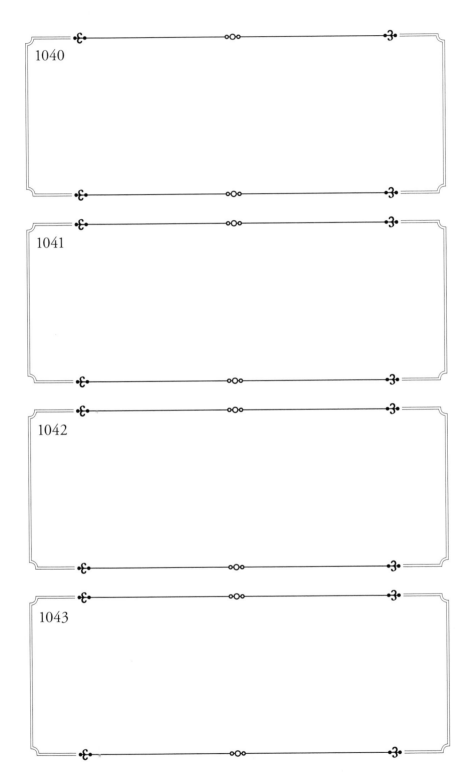

1040

1041

1042

1043

1044

1045

1046

1047

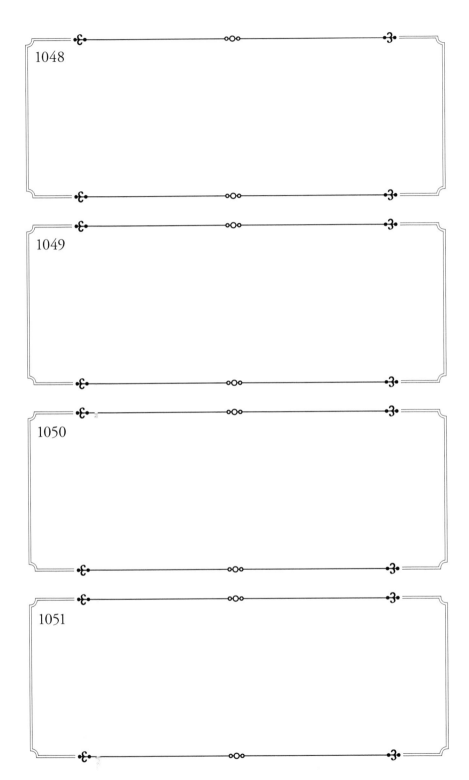

1048

1049

1050

1051

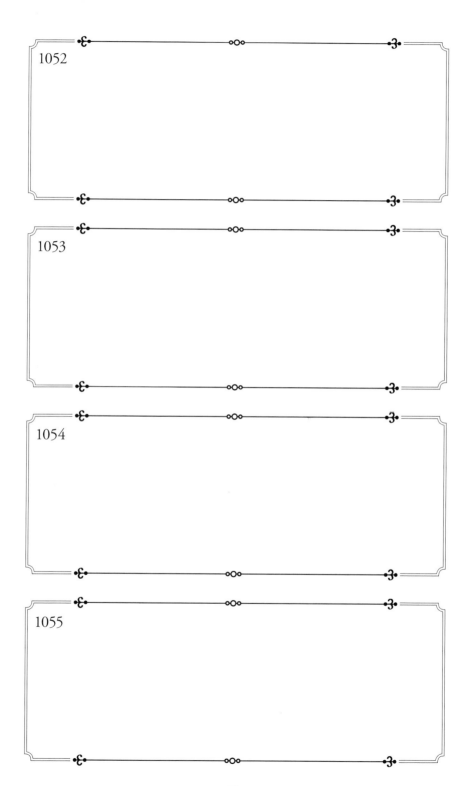

1052

1053

1054

1055

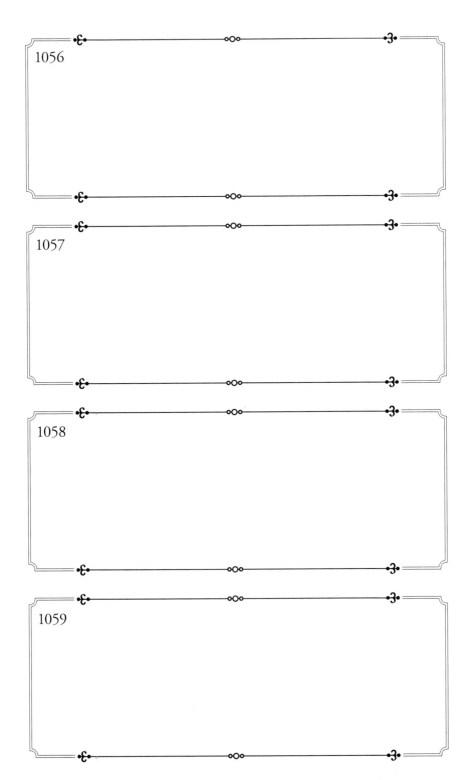

1056

1057

1058

1059

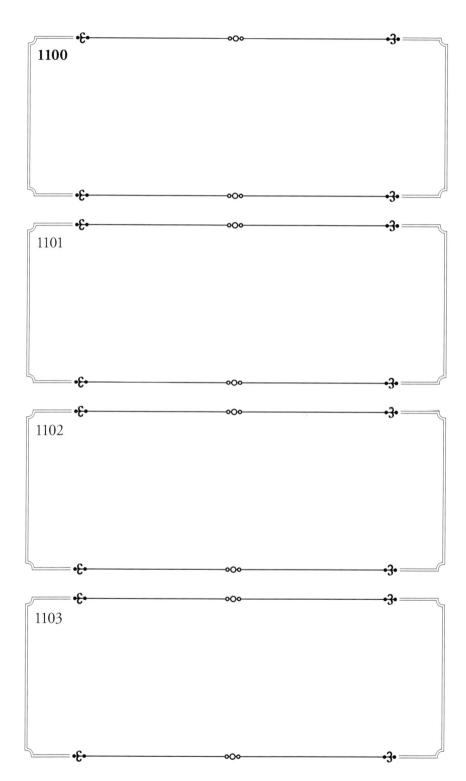

1100

1101

1102

1103

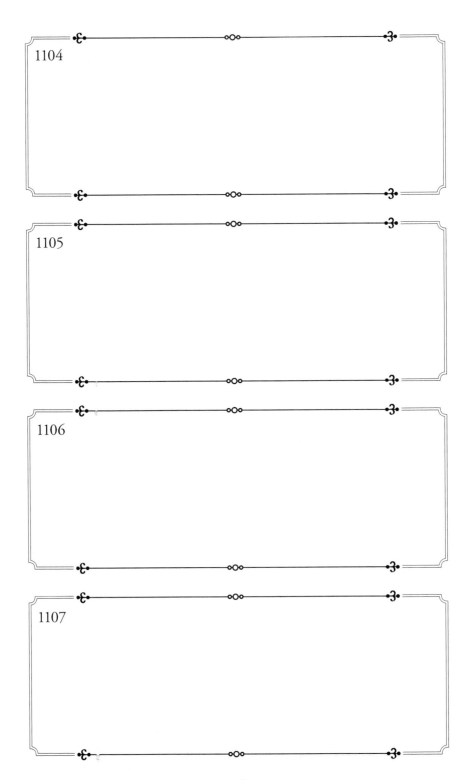

1104

1105

1106

1107

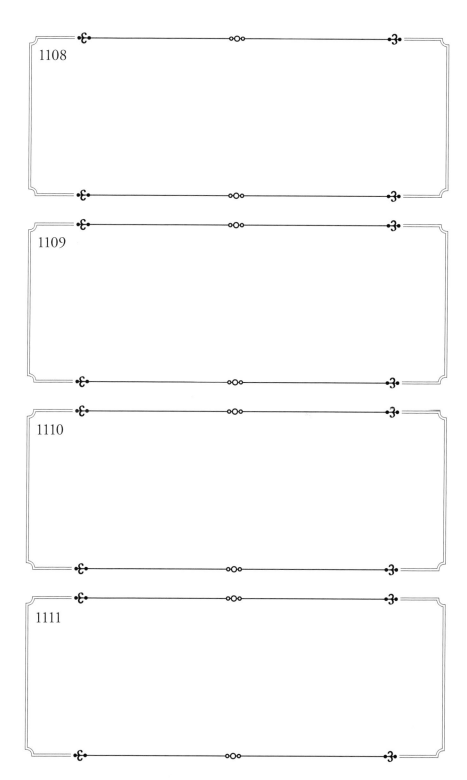

1108

1109

1110

1111

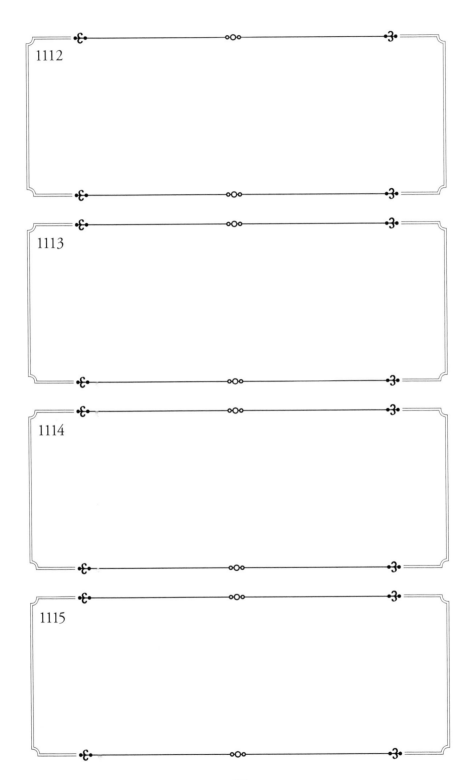

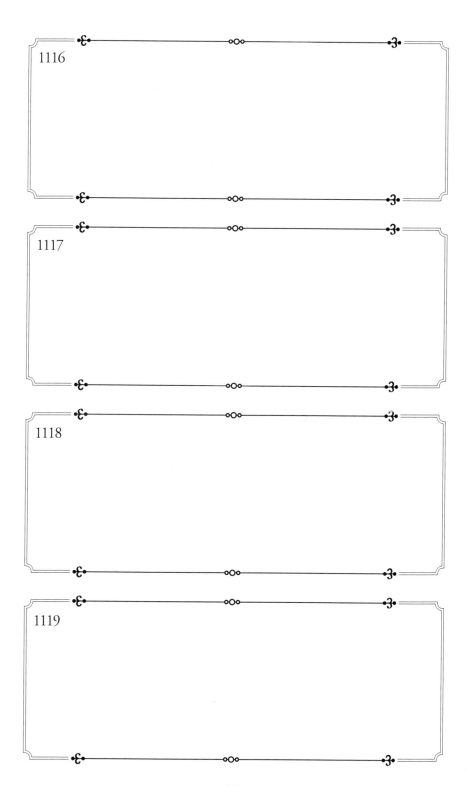

1116

1117

1118

1119

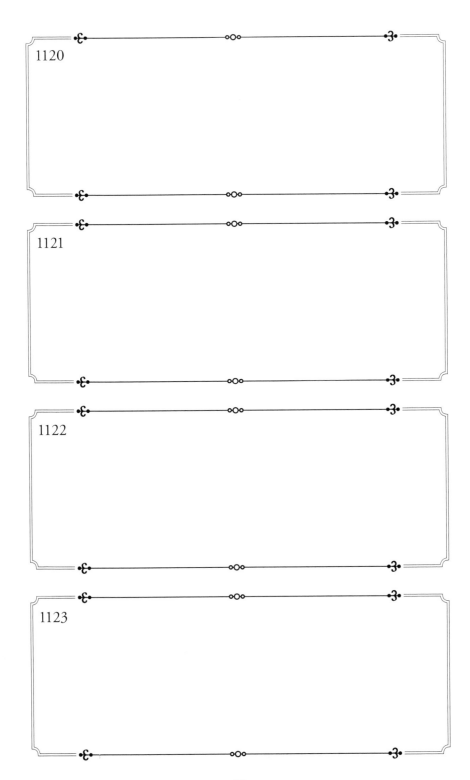

1120

1121

1122

1123

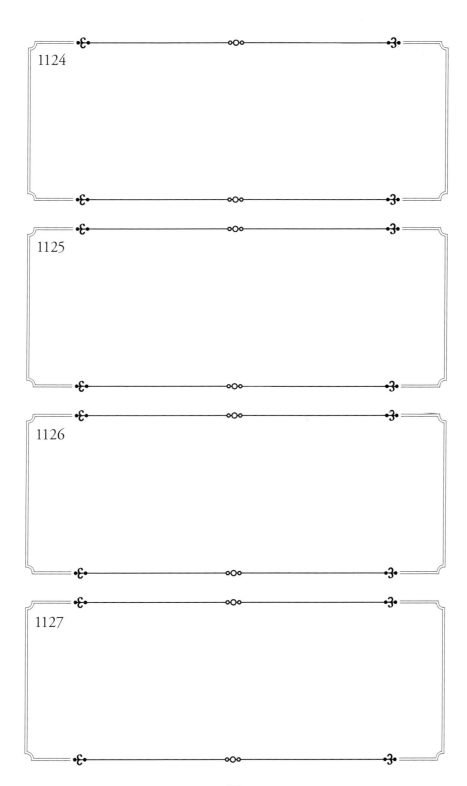

1124

1125

1126

1127

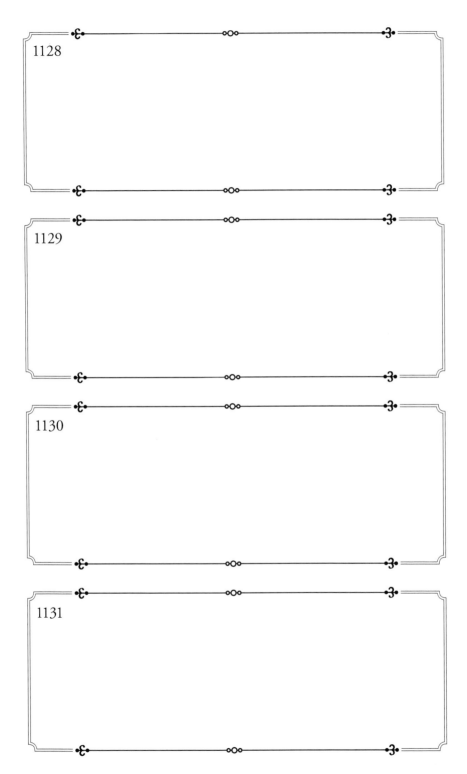

1128

1129

1130

1131

1132

1133

1134

1135

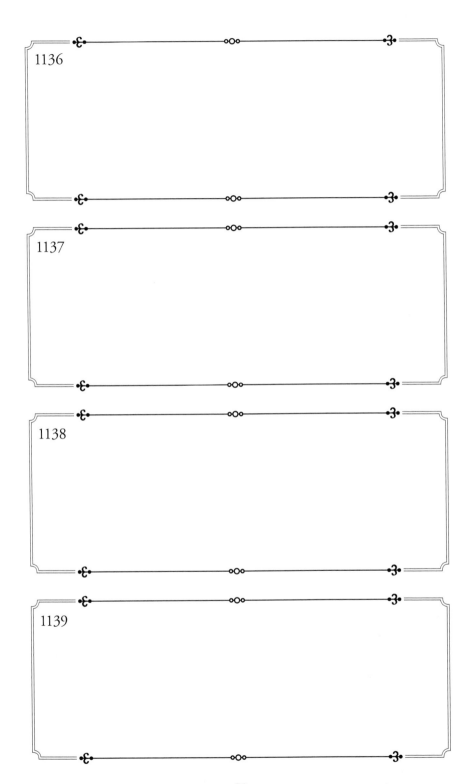

1136

1137

1138

1139

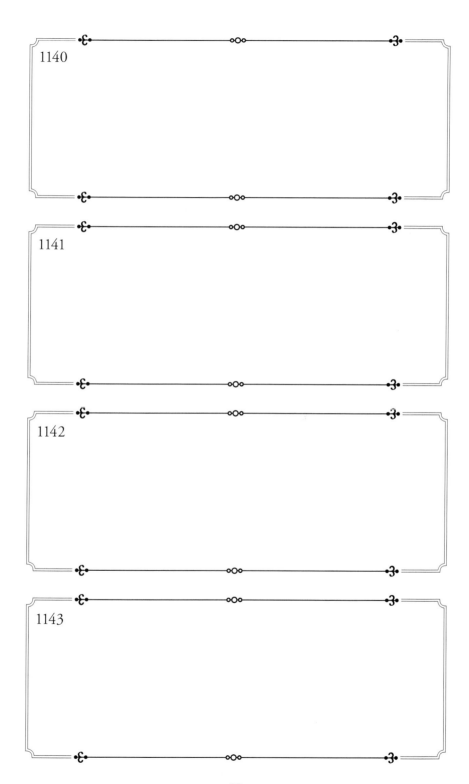

1140

1141

1142

1143

1144

1145

1146

1147

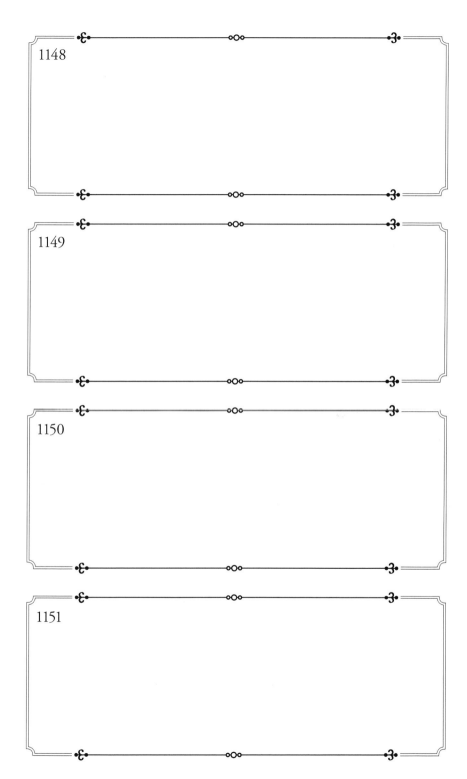

1148

1149

1150

1151

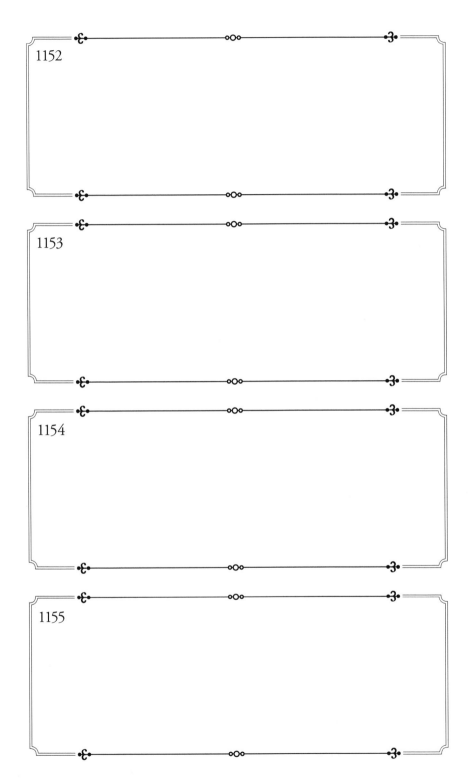

1152

1153

1154

1155

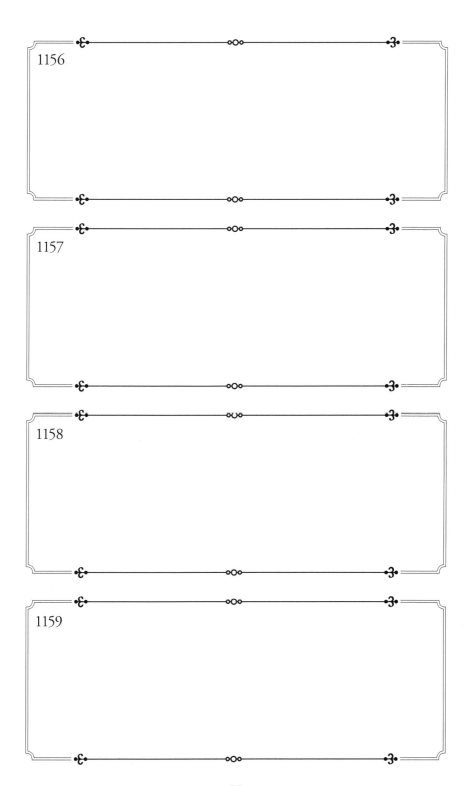

1156

1157

1158

1159

1200

1201

1202

1203

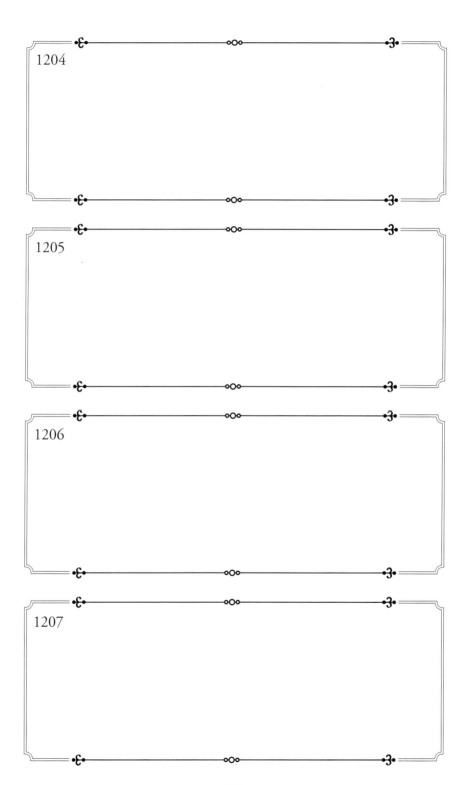

1204

1205

1206

1207

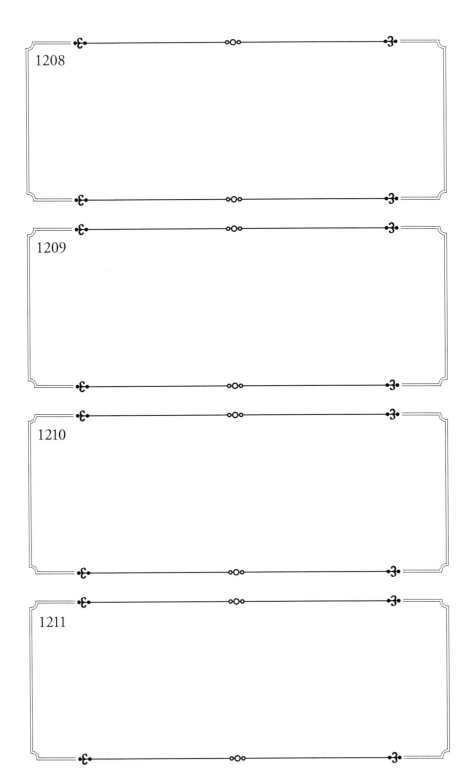

1208

1209

1210

1211

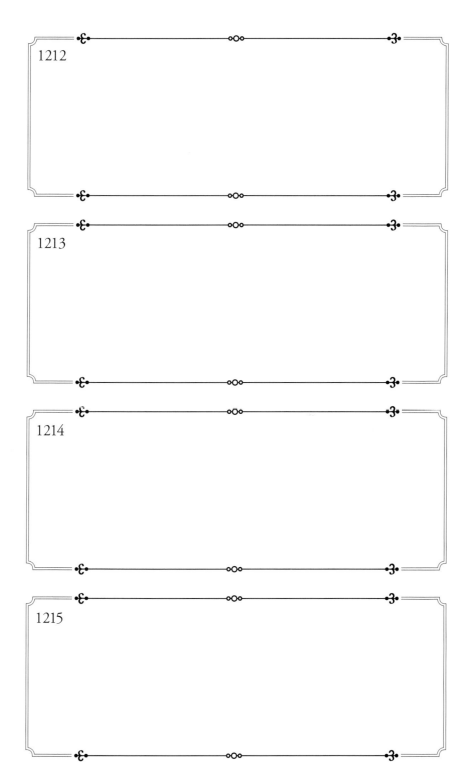

1212

1213

1214

1215

1216

1217

1218

1219

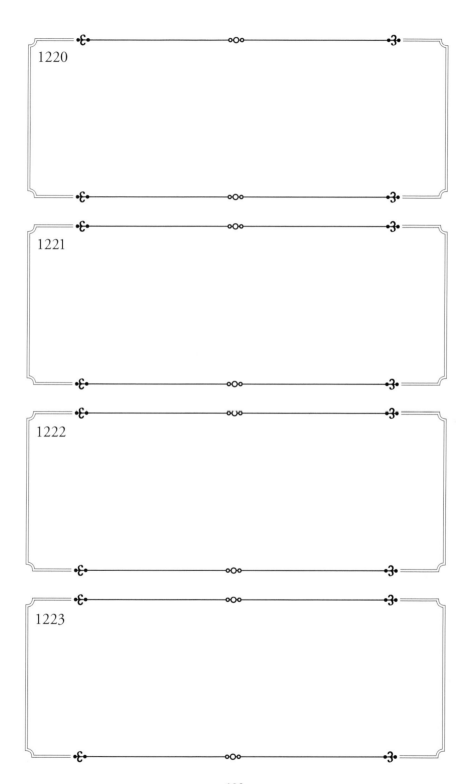

1220

1221

1222

1223

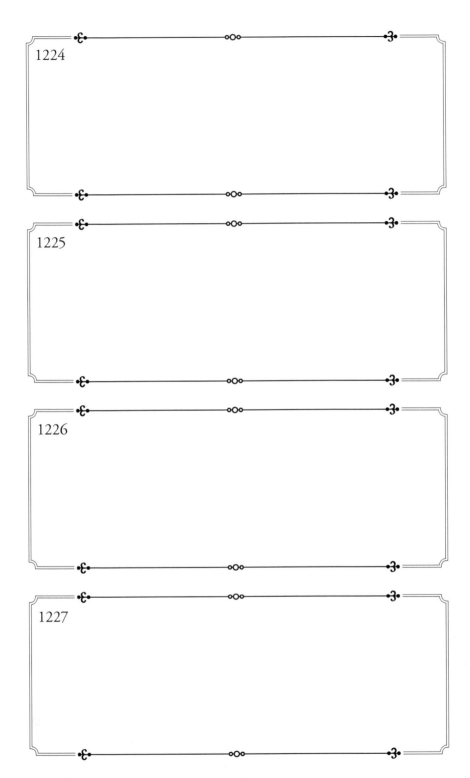

1224

1225

1226

1227

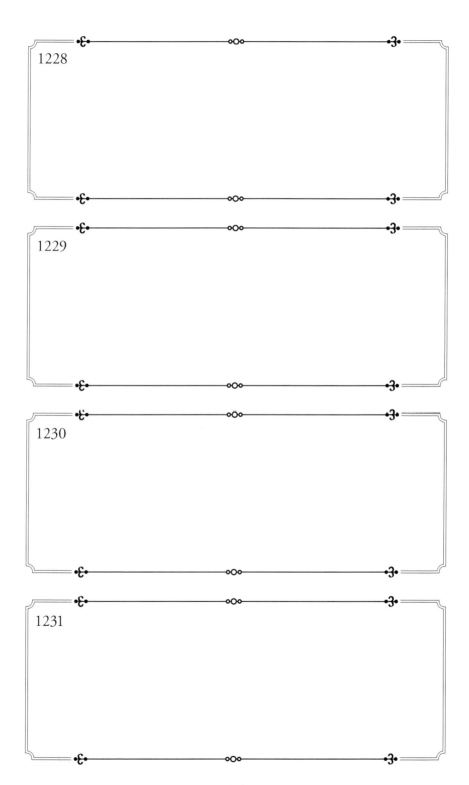

1228

1229

1230

1231

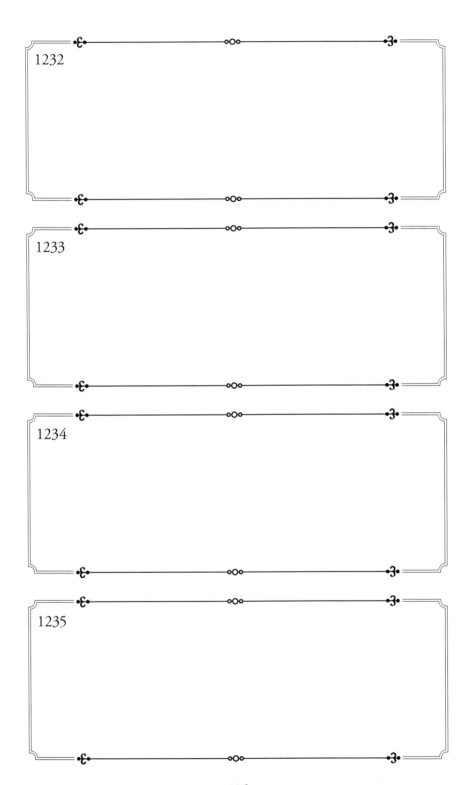

1232

1233

1234

1235

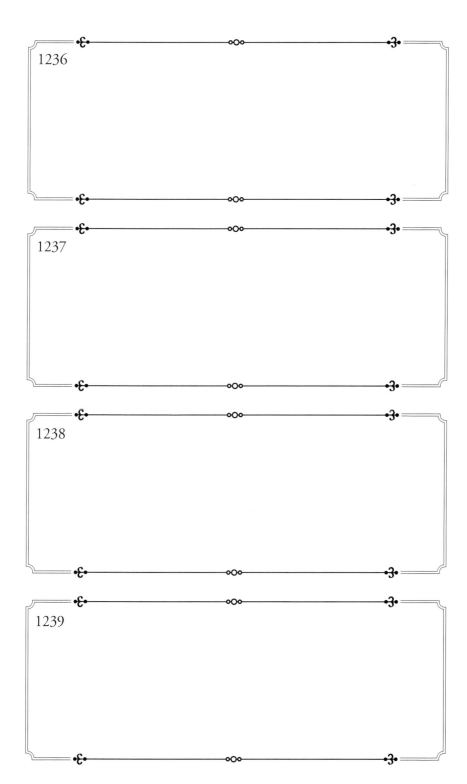

1236

1237

1238

1239

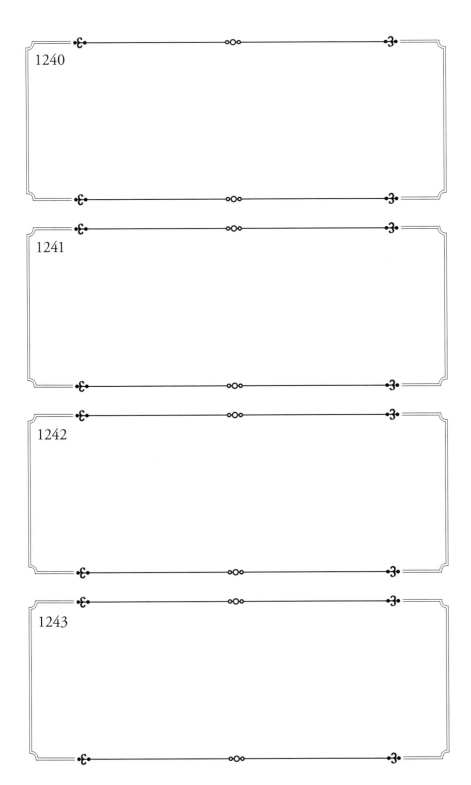

1240

1241

1242

1243

1244

1245

1246

1247

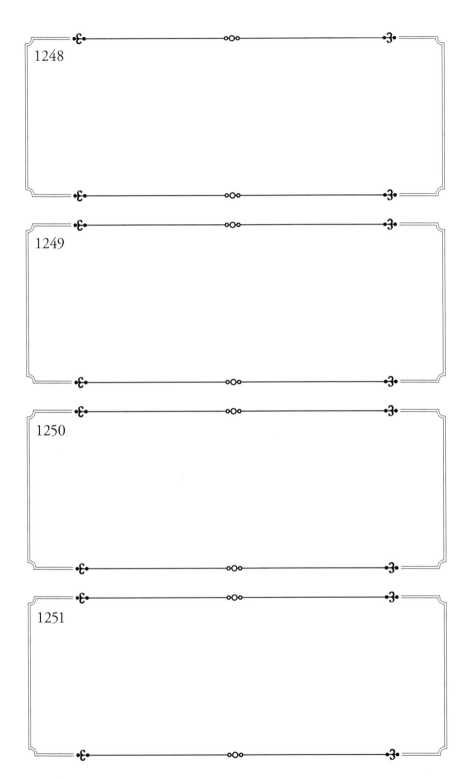

1248

1249

1250

1251

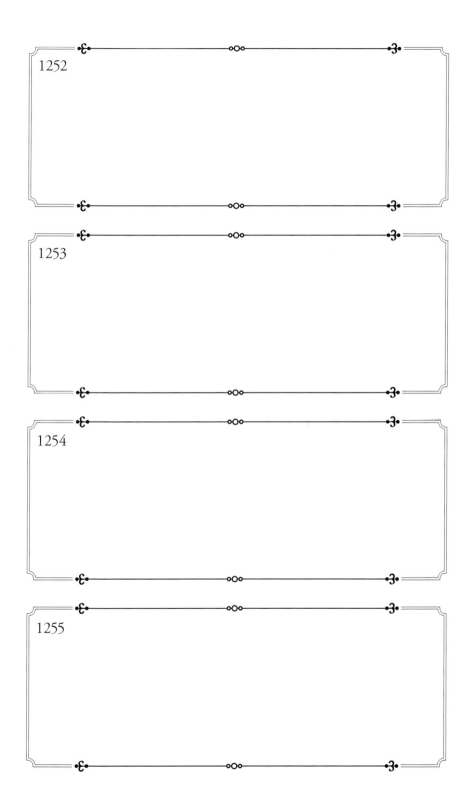

1252

1253

1254

1255

1256

1257

1258

1259

1300

1301

1302

1303

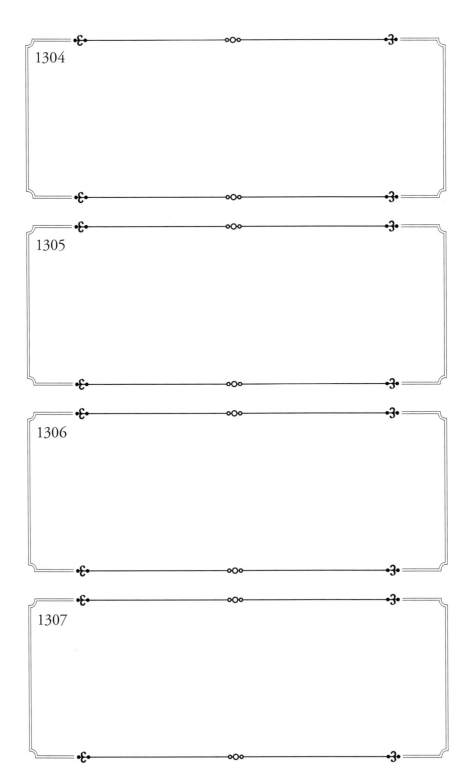

1304

1305

1306

1307

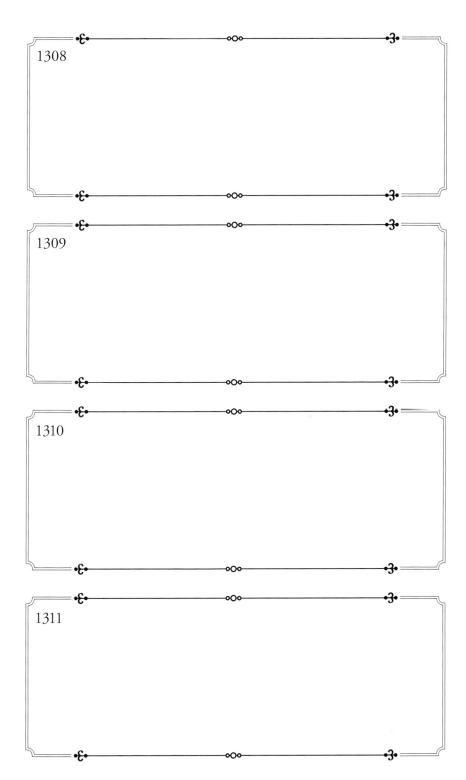

1308

1309

1310

1311

1312

1313

1314

1315

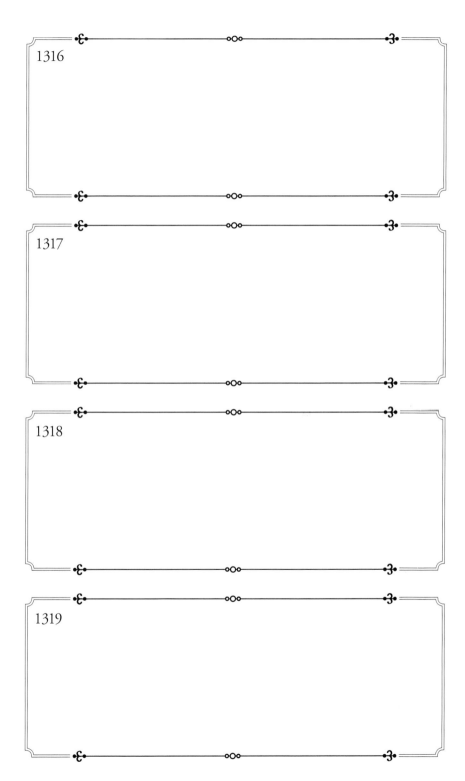

1316

1317

1318

1319

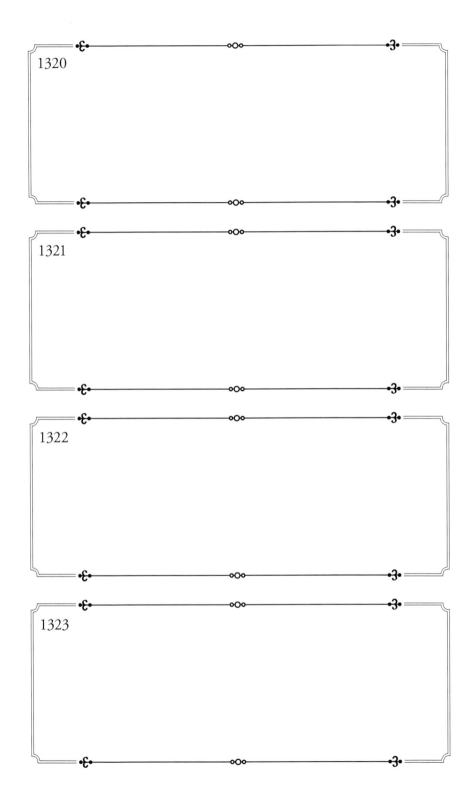

1320

1321

1322

1323

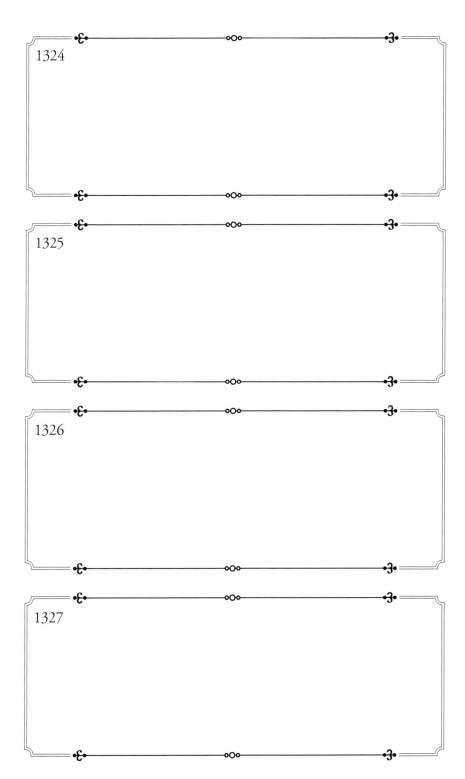

1324

1325

1326

1327

1328

1329

1330

1331

1332

1333

1334

1335

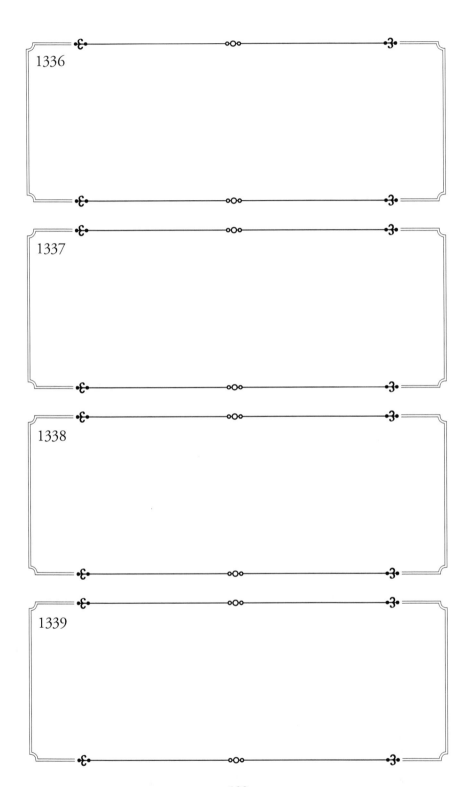

1336

1337

1338

1339

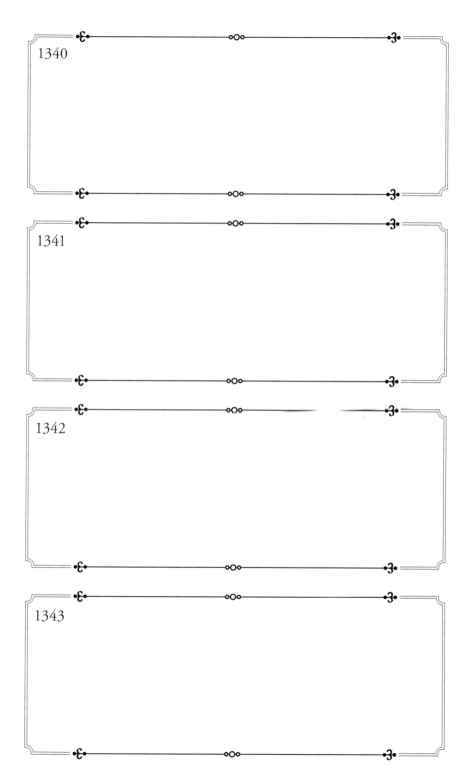

1340

1341

1342

1343

1344

1345

1346

1347

1348

1349

1350

1351

1352

1353

1354

1355

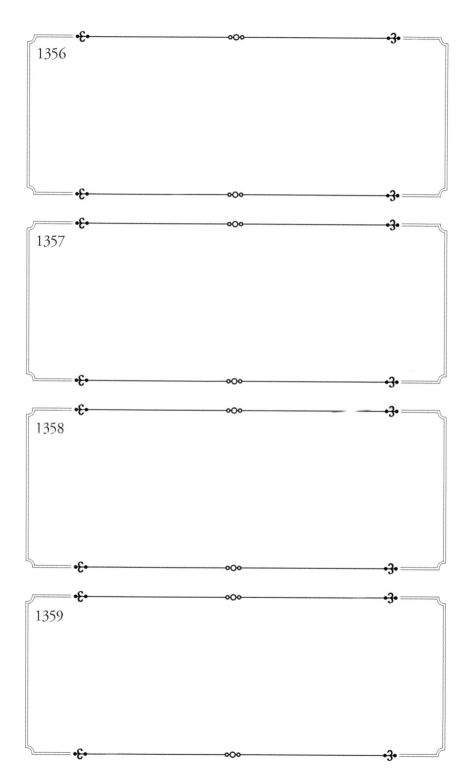

1356

1357

1358

1359

1400

1401

1402

1403

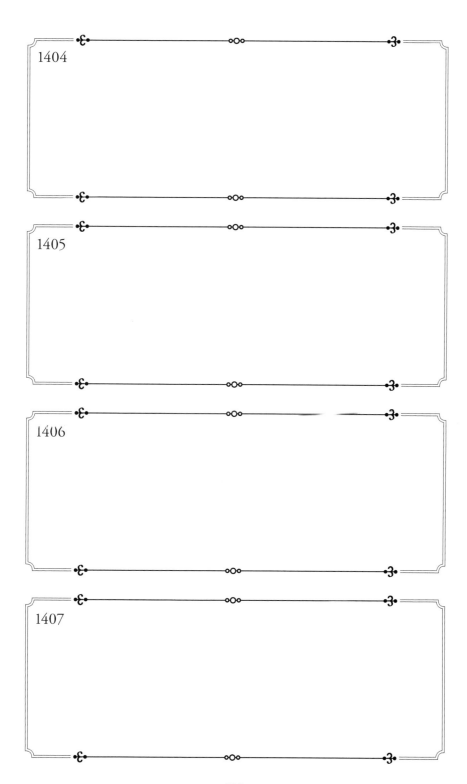

1404

1405

1406

1407

1408

1409

1410

1411

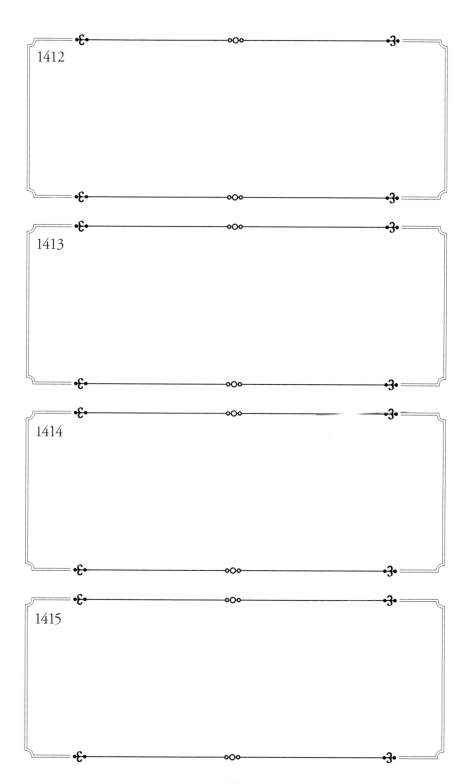

1412

1413

1414

1415

1416

1417

1418

1419

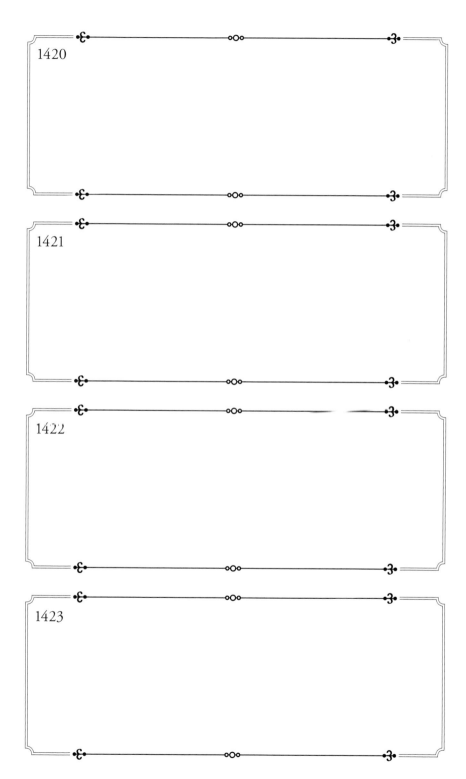

1420

1421

1422

1423

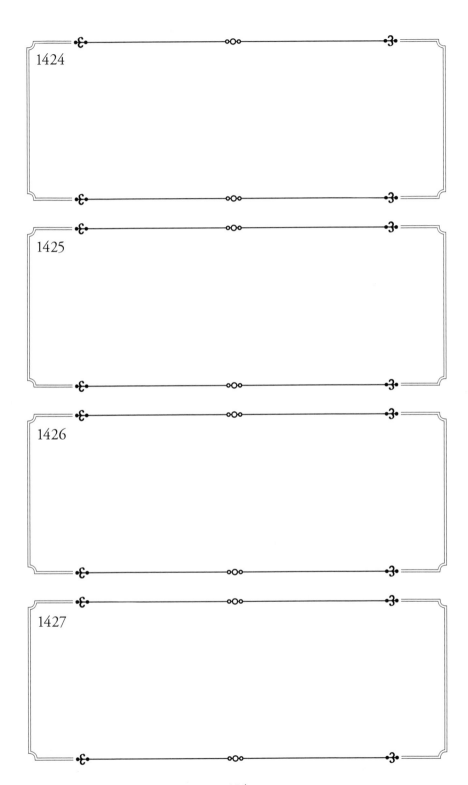

1424

1425

1426

1427

1428

1429

1430

1431

1432

1433

1434

1435

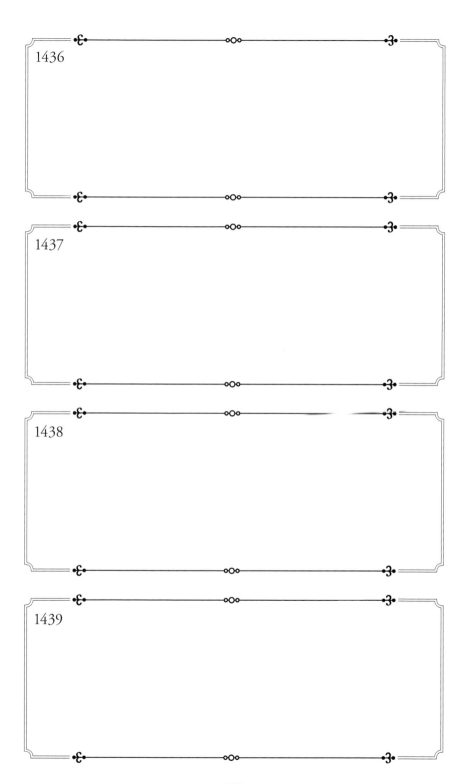

1436

1437

1438

1439

1440

1441

1442

1443

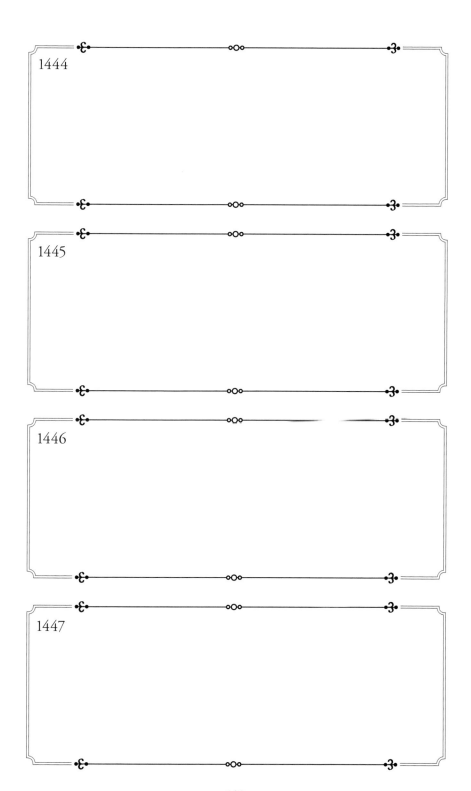

1444

1445

1446

1447

1448

1449

1450

1451

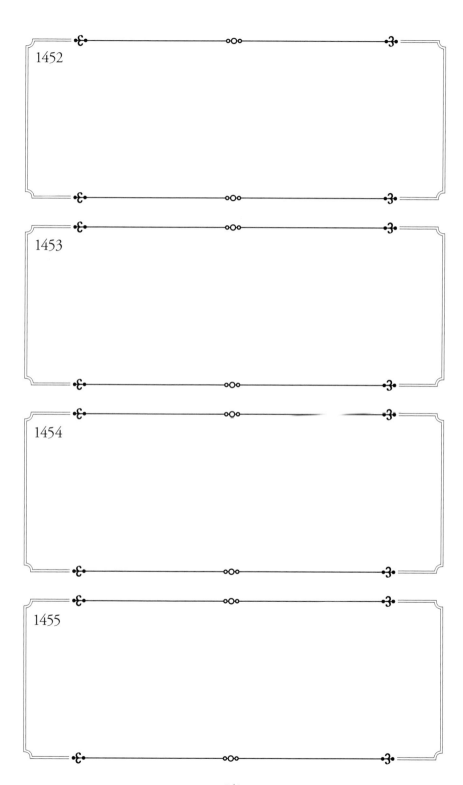

1452

1453

1454

1455

1456

1457

1458

1459

1500

1501

1502

1503

1504

1505

1506

1507

1508

1509

1510

1511

1512

1513

1514

1515

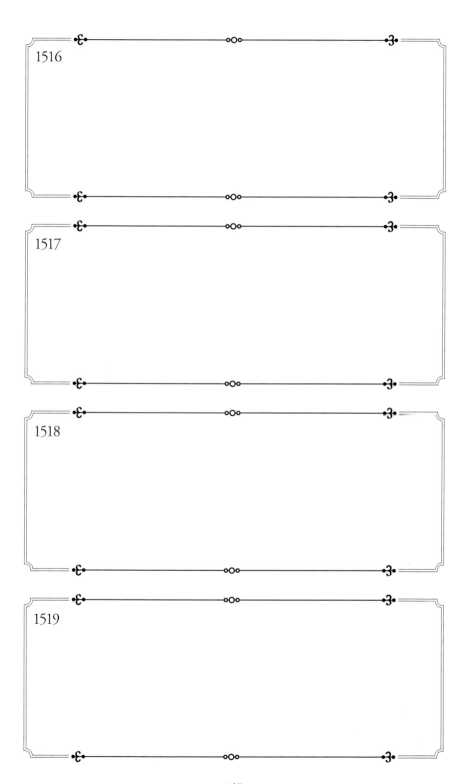

1516

1517

1518

1519

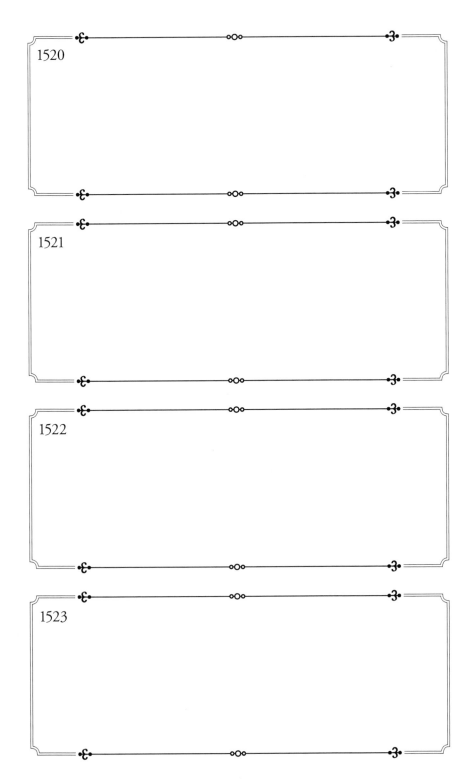

1520

1521

1522

1523

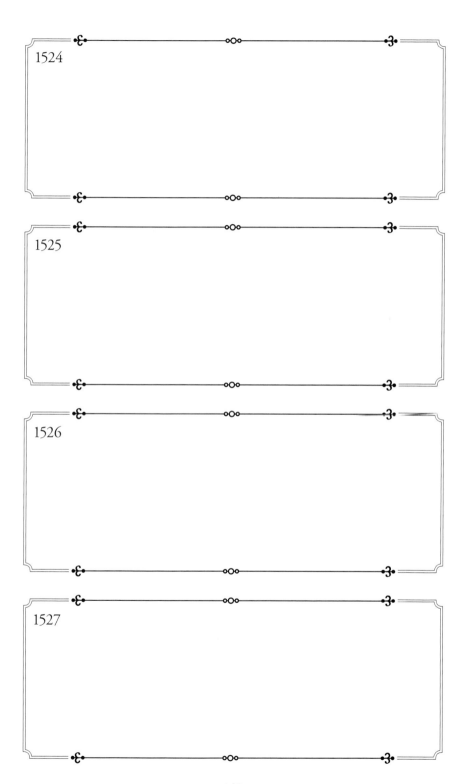

1524

1525

1526

1527

1528

1529

1530

1531

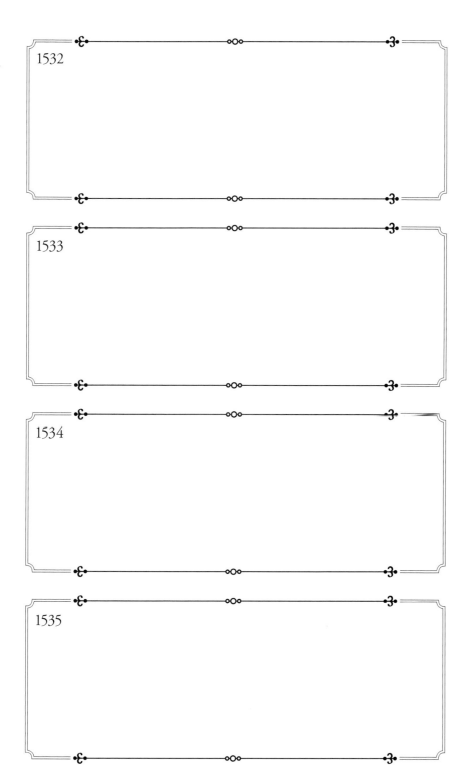

1532

1533

1534

1535

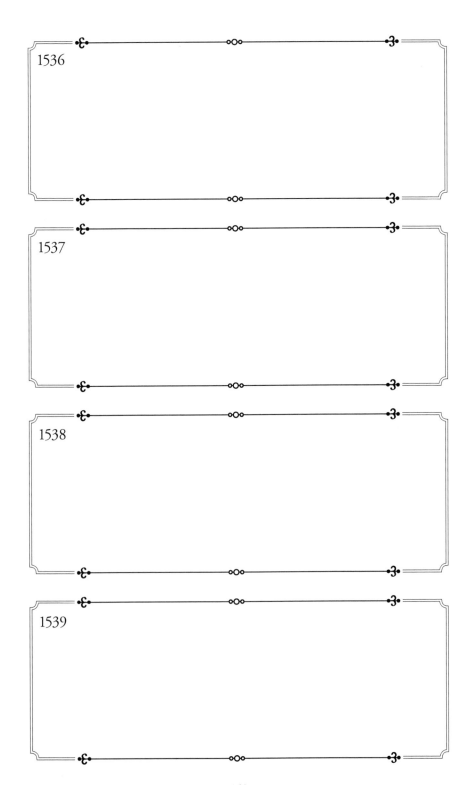

1536

1537

1538

1539

1540

1541

1542

1543

1544

1545

1546

1547

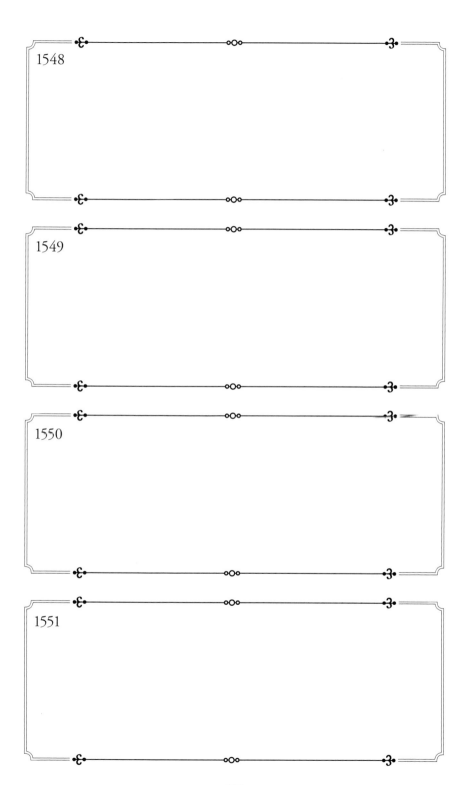

1548

1549

1550

1551

1552

1553

1554

1555

156

1556

1557

1558

1559

1600

1601

1602

1603

1604

1605

1606

1607

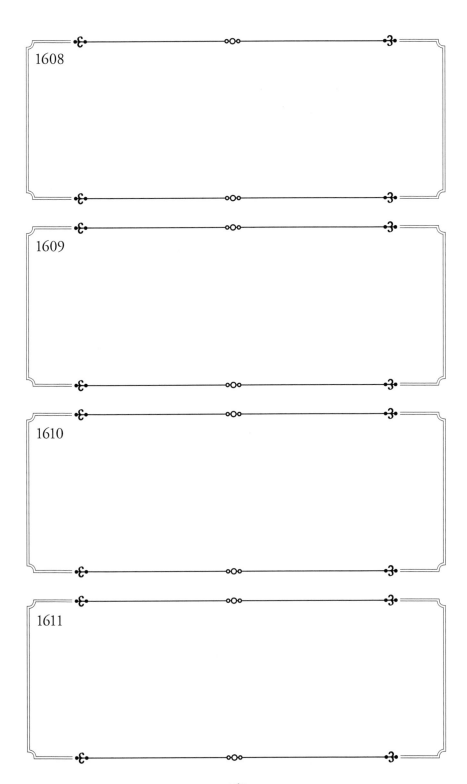

1608

1609

1610

1611

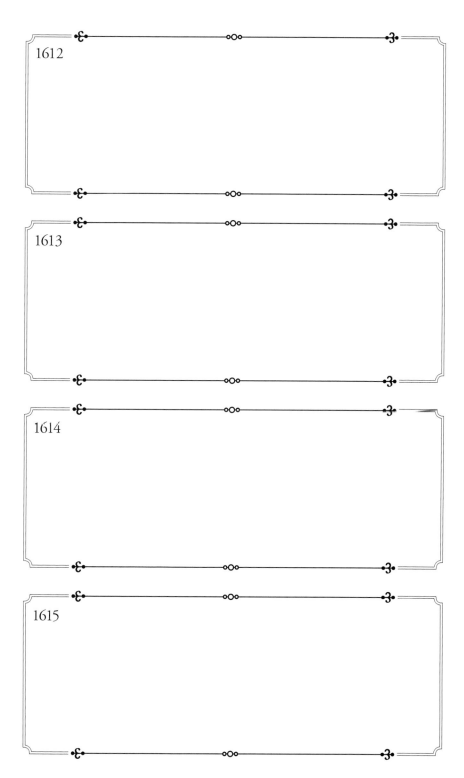

1612

1613

1614

1615

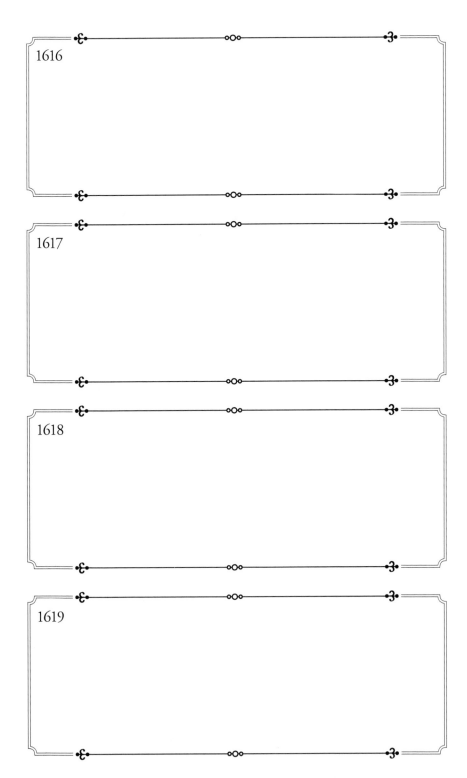

1616

1617

1618

1619

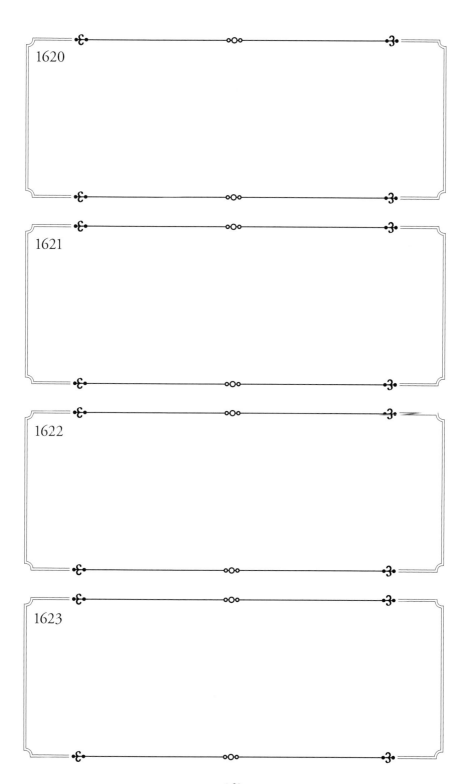

1620

1621

1622

1623

1624

1625

1626

1627

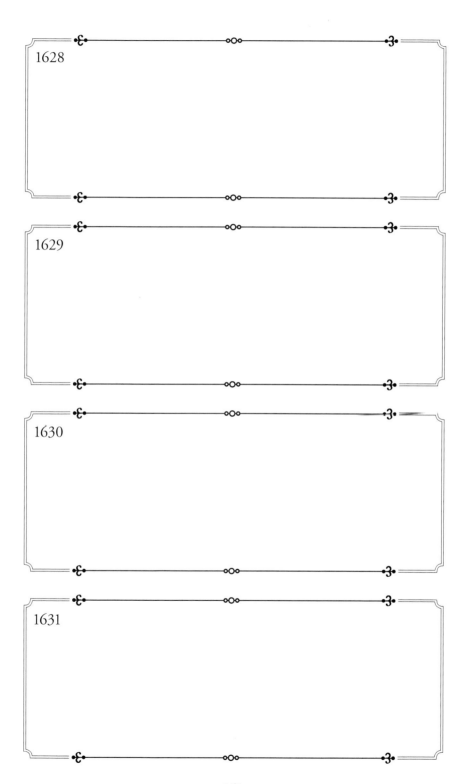

1628

1629

1630

1631

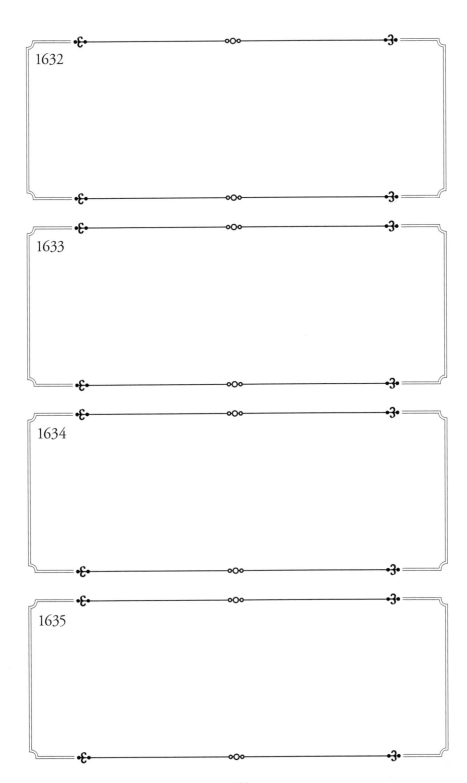

1632

1633

1634

1635

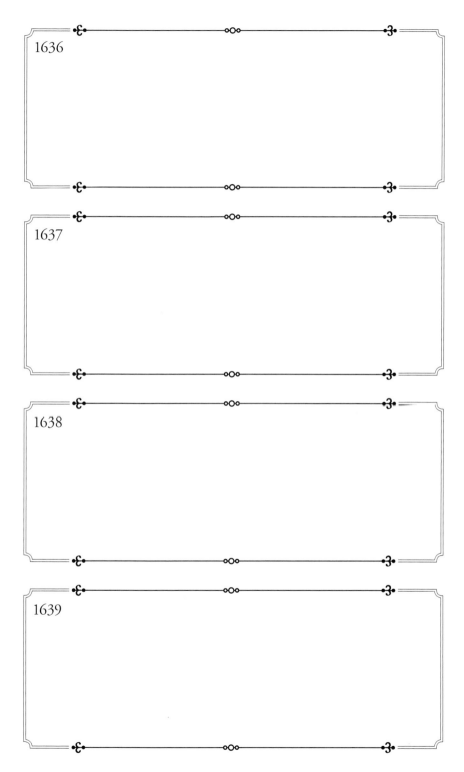

1636

1637

1638

1639

1640

1641

1642

1643

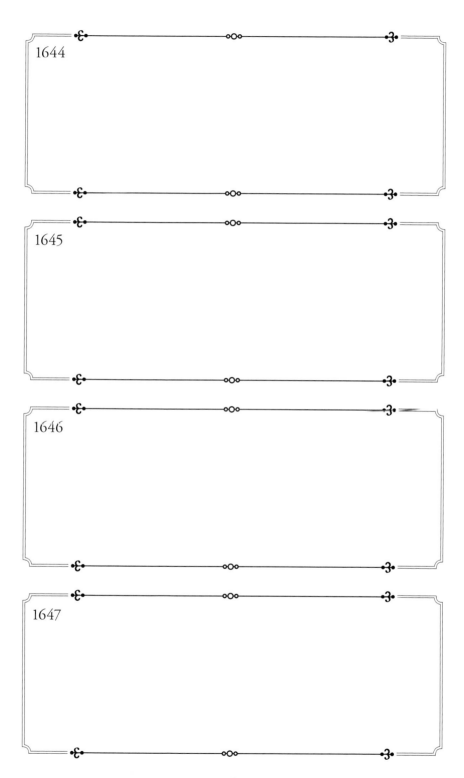

1644

1645

1646

1647

1648

1649

1650

1651

1652

1653

1654

1655

1656

1657

1658

1659

1700

1701

1702

1703

1704

1705

1706

1707

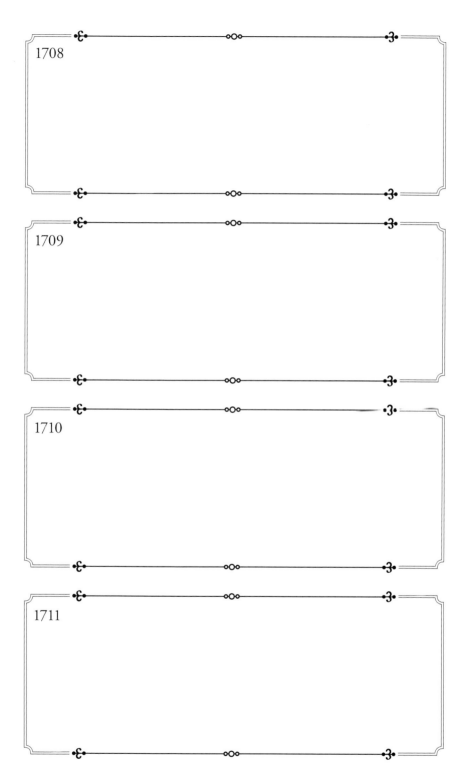

1708

1709

1710

1711

1712

1713

1714

1715

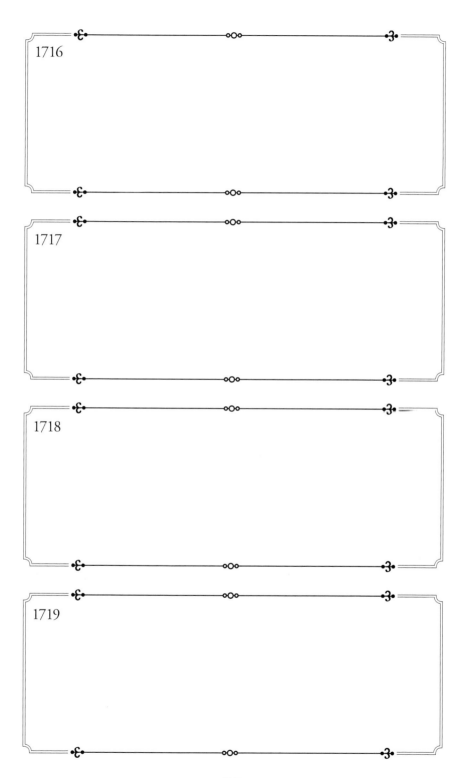

1716

1717

1718

1719

1720

1721

1722

1723

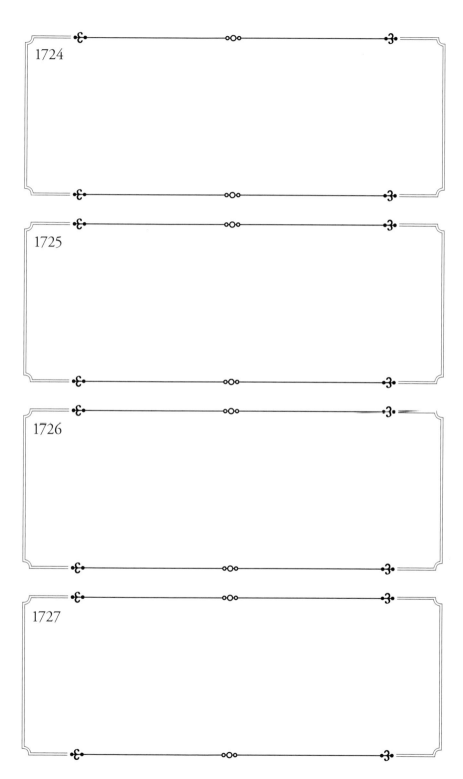

1724

1725

1726

1727

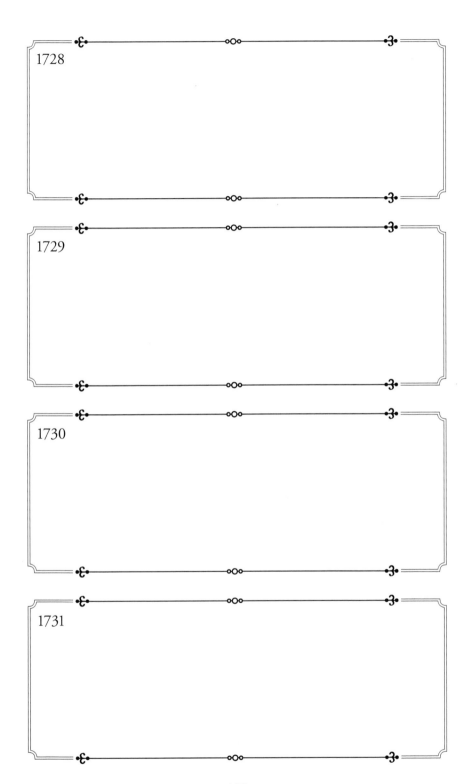

1728

1729

1730

1731

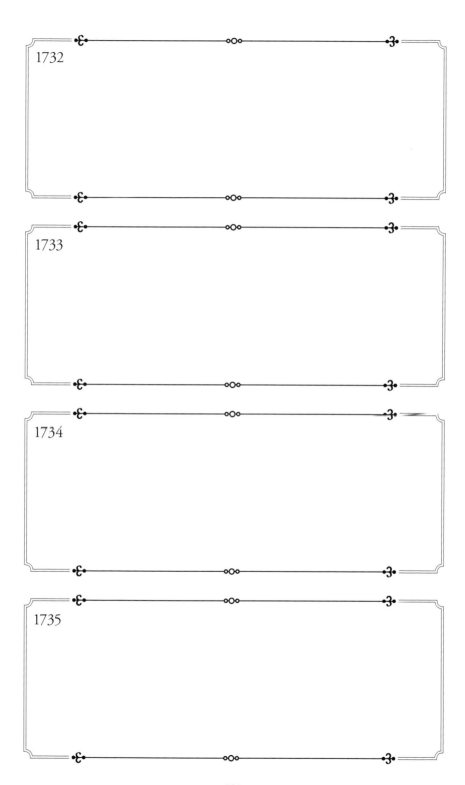

1732

1733

1734

1735

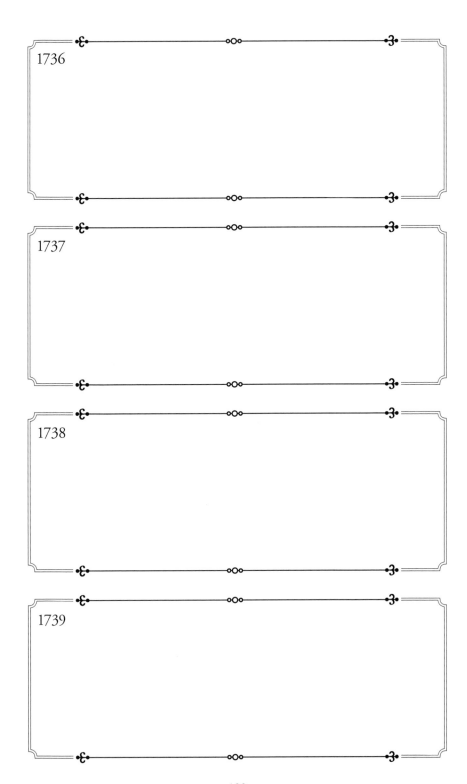

1736

1737

1738

1739

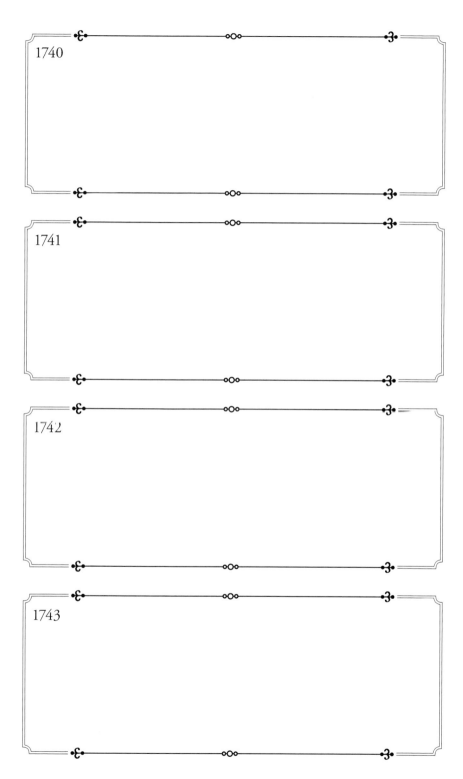

1740

1741

1742

1743

1744

1745

1746

1747

1748

1749

1750

1751

1752

1753

1754

1755

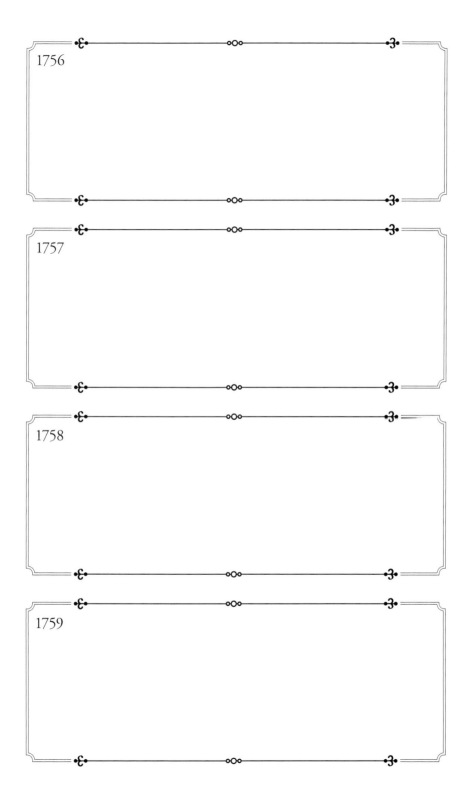

1756

1757

1758

1759

1800

1801

1802

1803

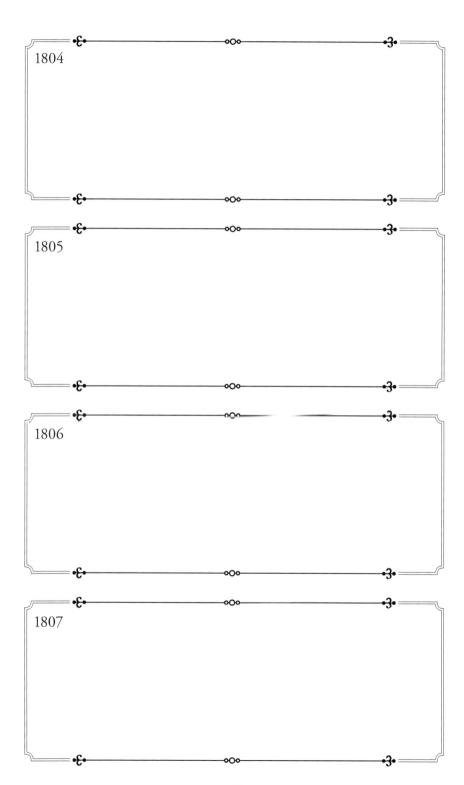

1804

1805

1806

1807

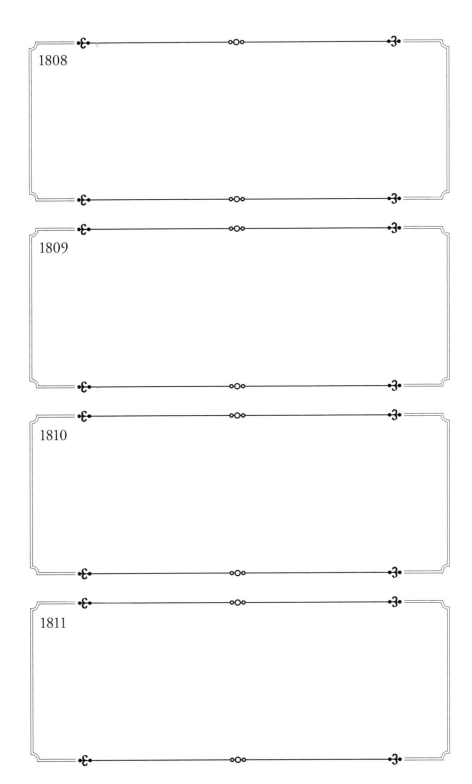

1808

1809

1810

1811

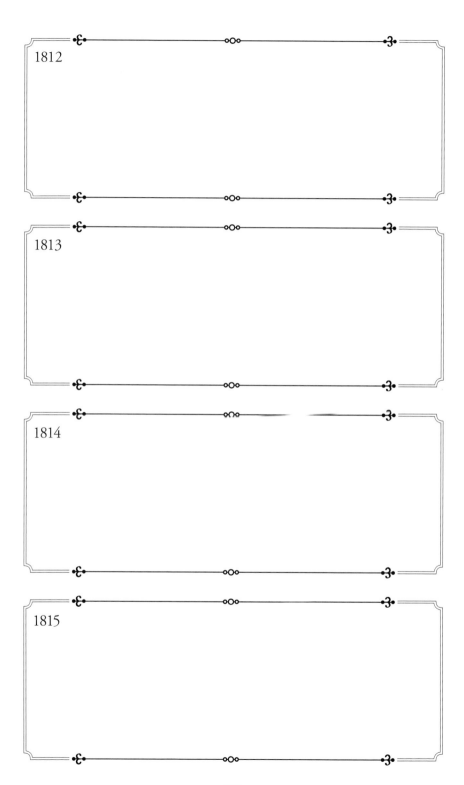

1812

1813

1814

1815

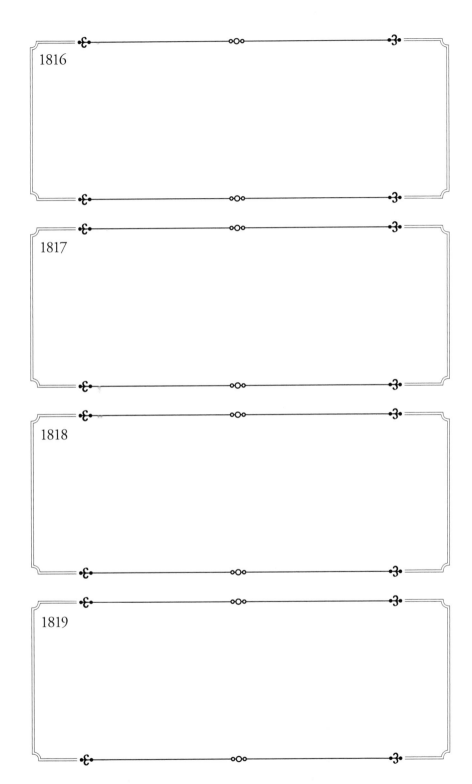

1816

1817

1818

1819

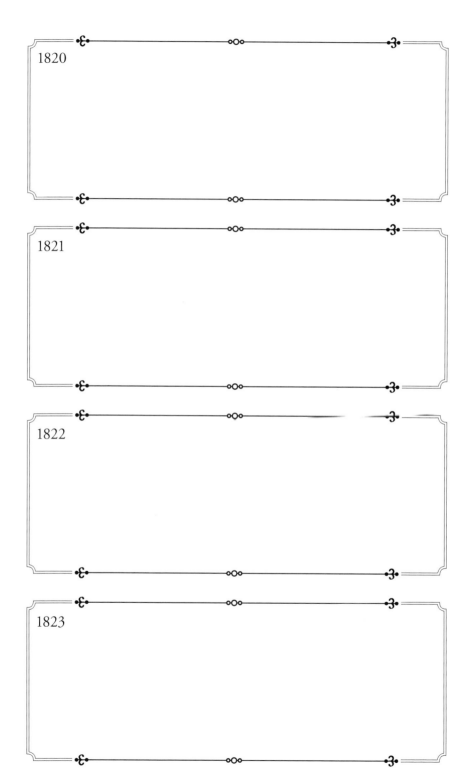

1820

1821

1822

1823

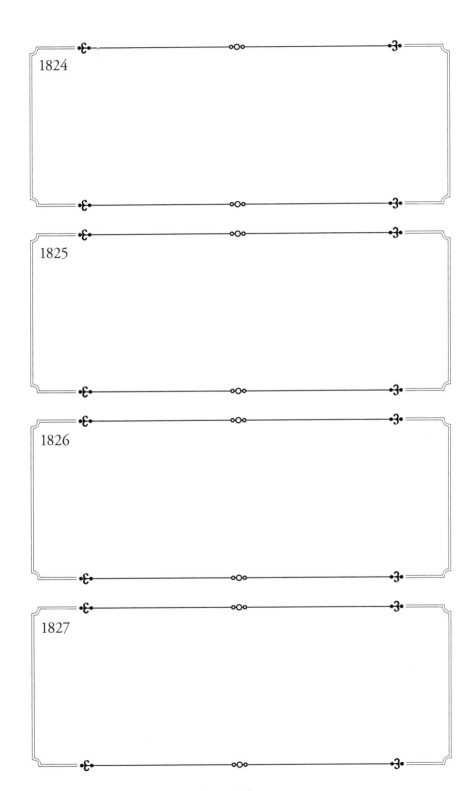

1824

1825

1826

1827

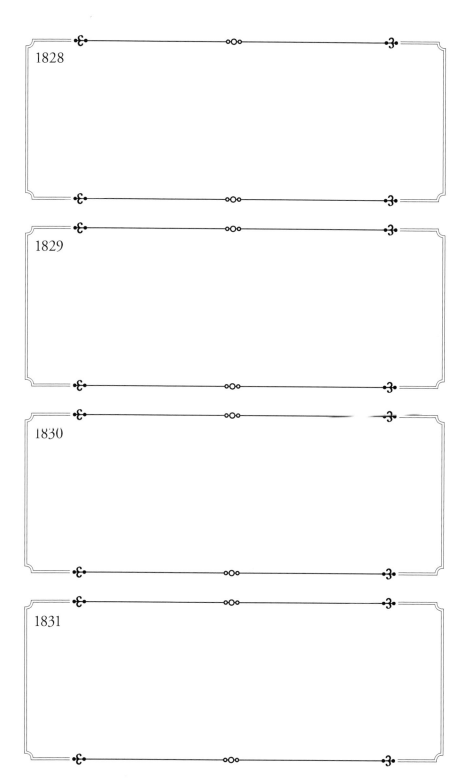

1828

1829

1830

1831

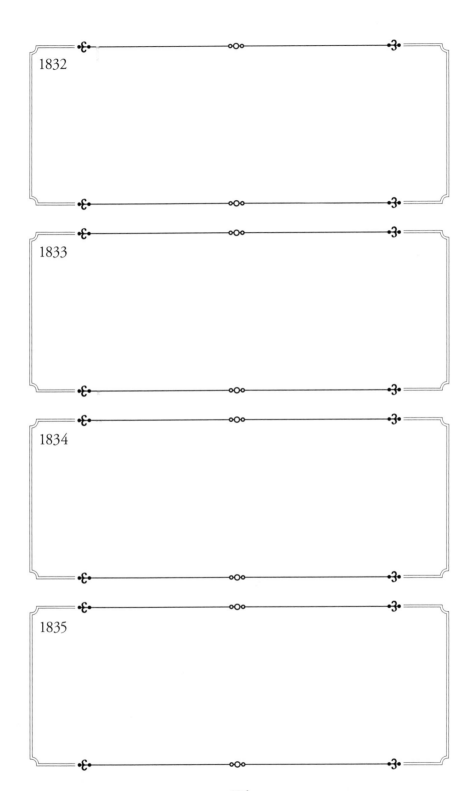

1832

1833

1834

1835

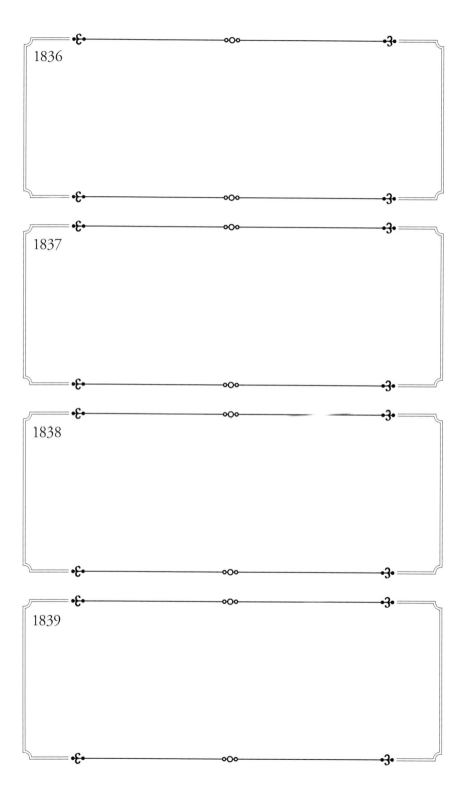

1836

1837

1838

1839

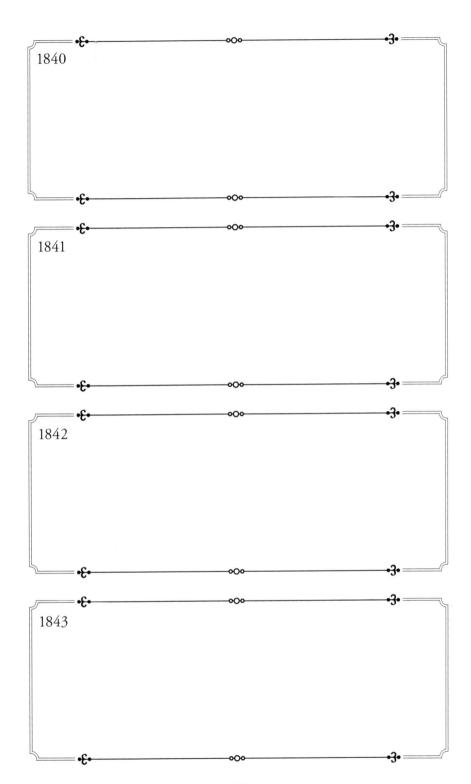

1840

1841

1842

1843

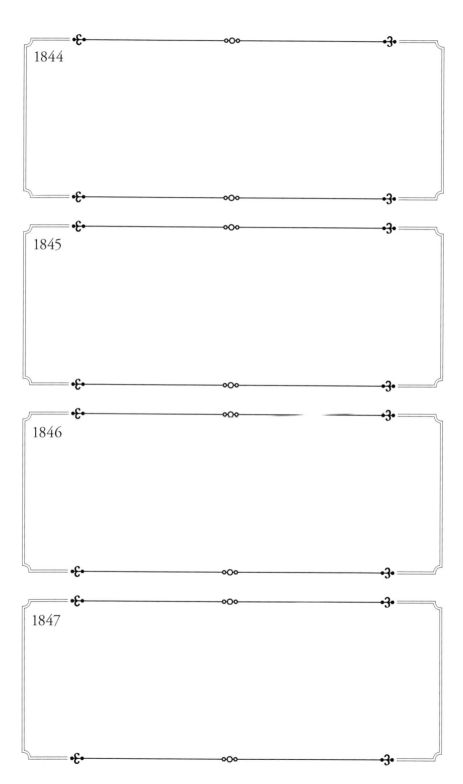

1844

1845

1846

1847

1848

1849

1850

1851

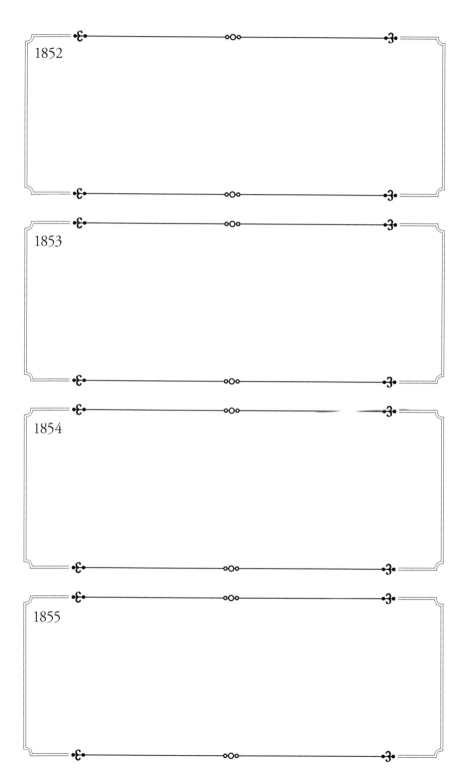

1852

1853

1854

1855

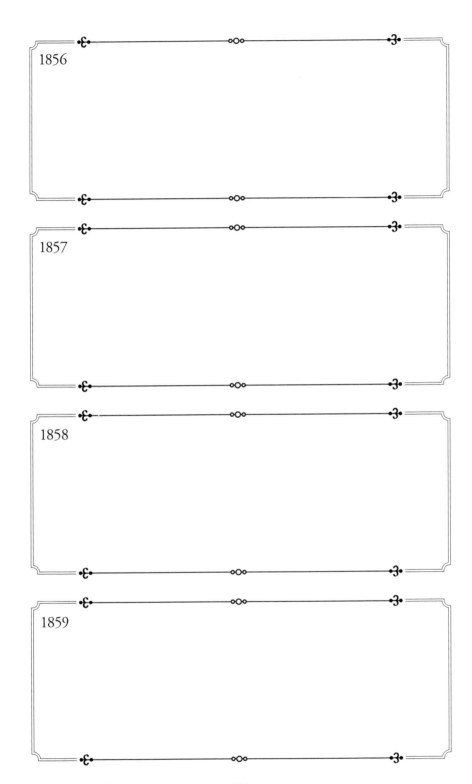

1856

1857

1858

1859

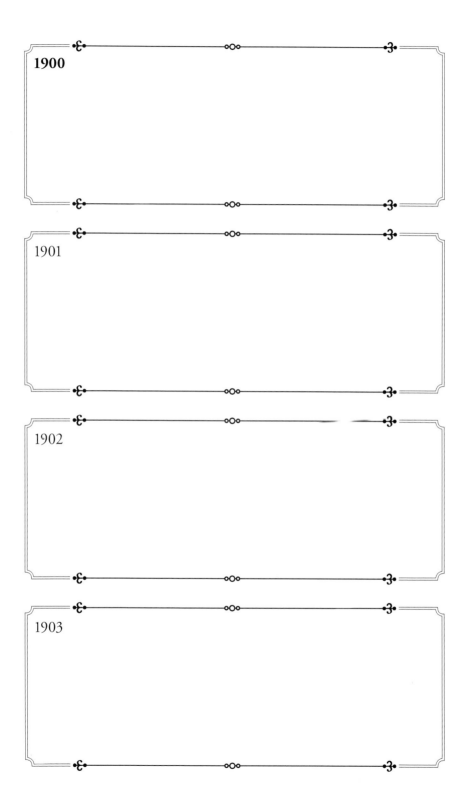

1900

1901

1902

1903

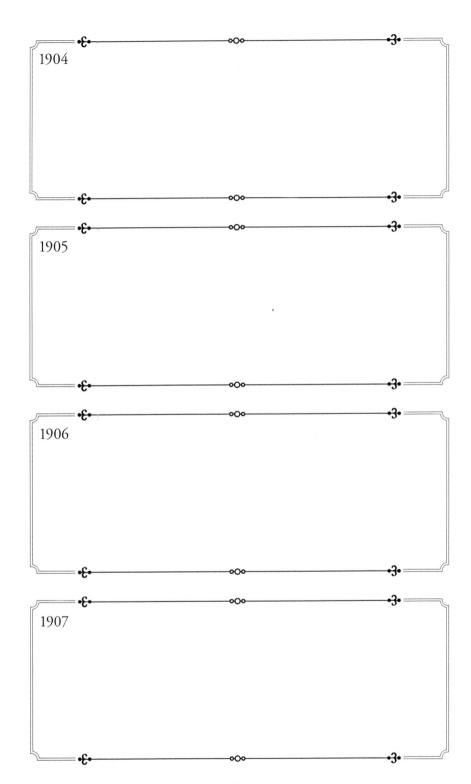

1904

1905

1906

1907

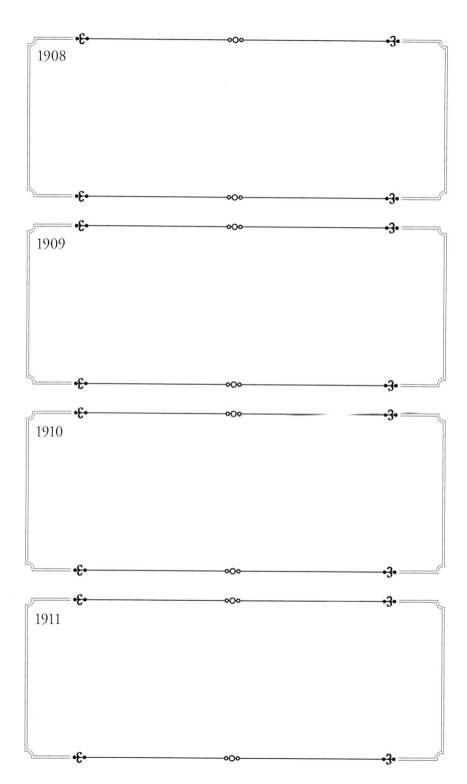

1908

1909

1910

1911

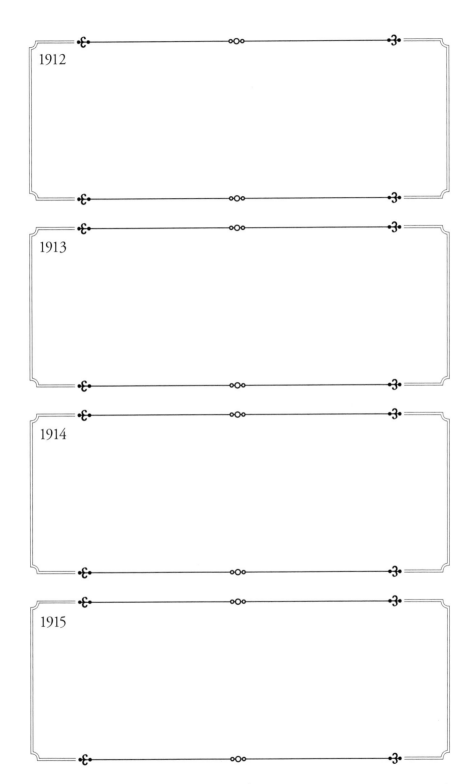

1912

1913

1914

1915

1916

1917

1918

1919

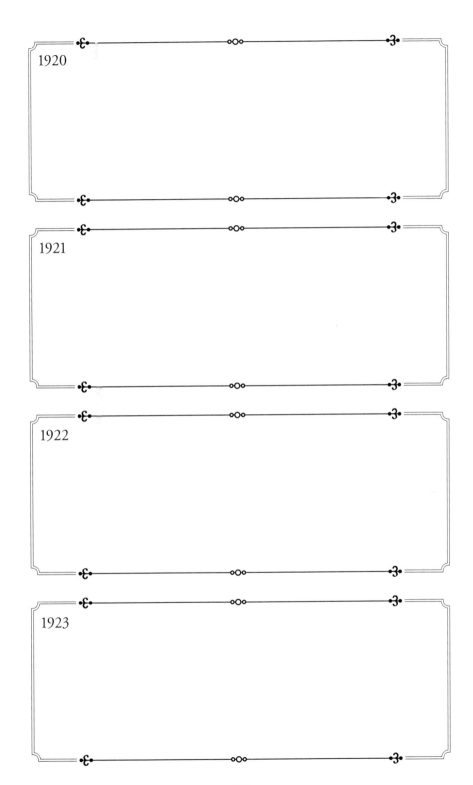

1920

1921

1922

1923

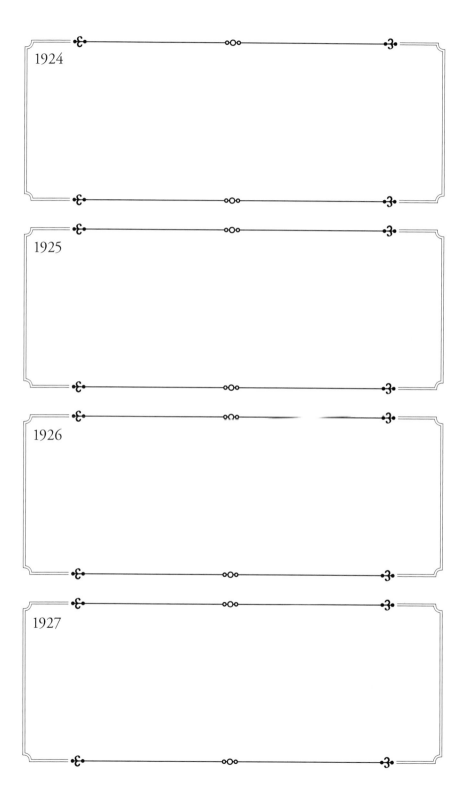

1924

1925

1926

1927

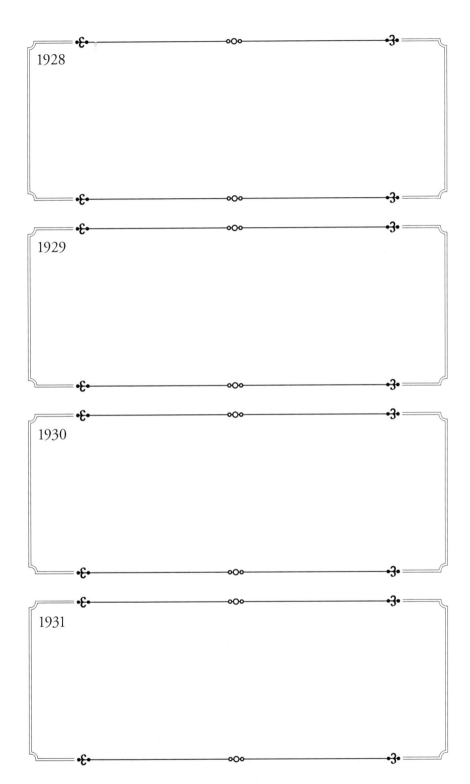

1928

1929

1930

1931

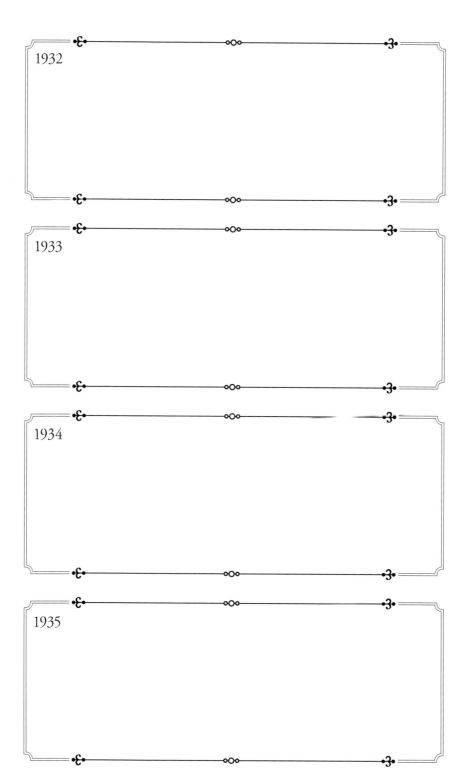

1932

1933

1934

1935

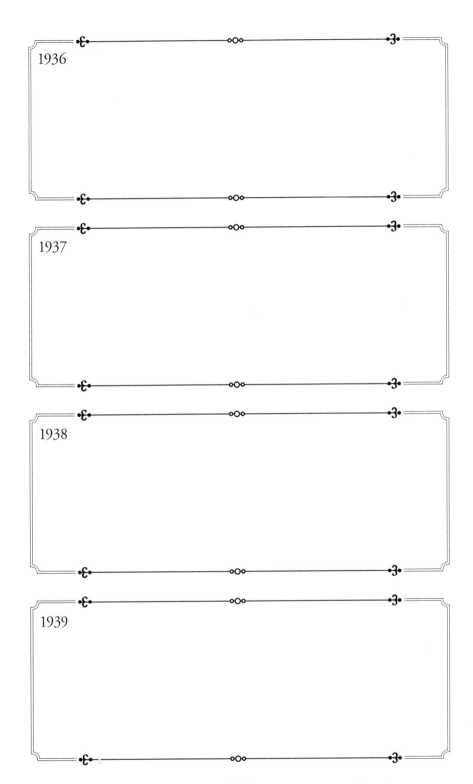

1936

1937

1938

1939

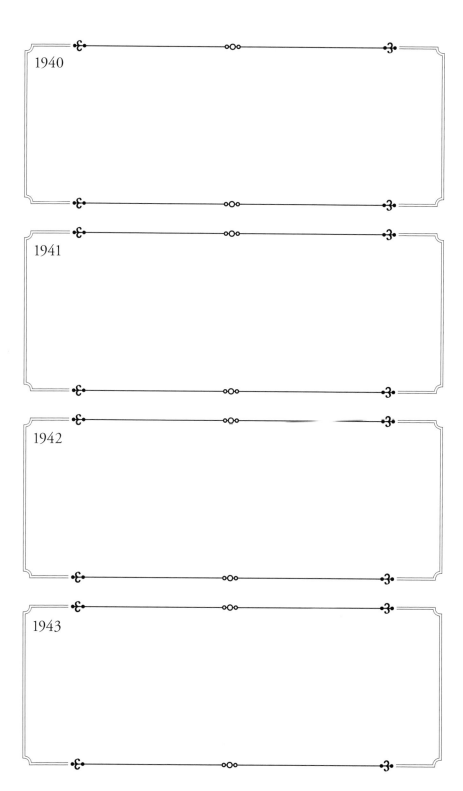

1940

1941

1942

1943

1944

1945

1946

1947

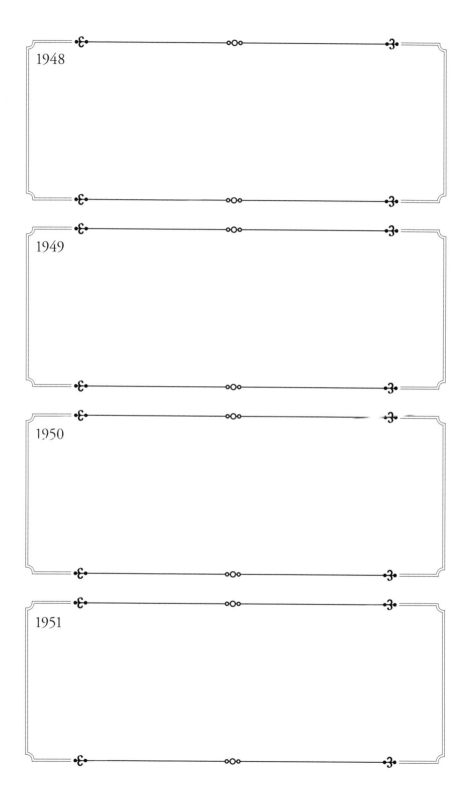

1948

1949

1950

1951

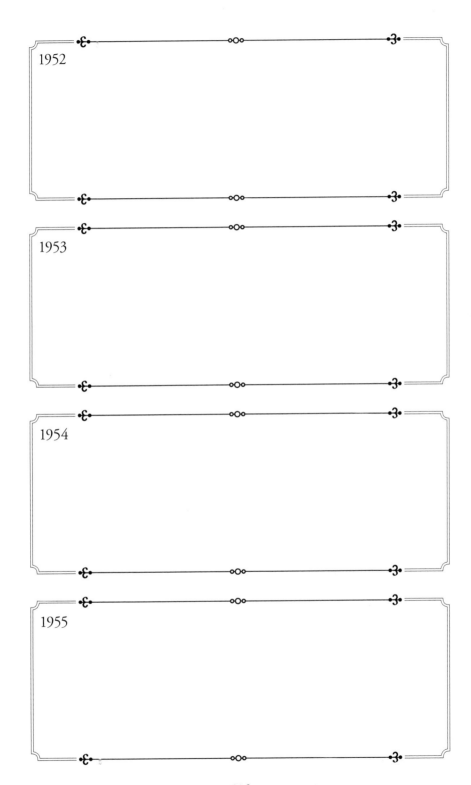

1952

1953

1954

1955

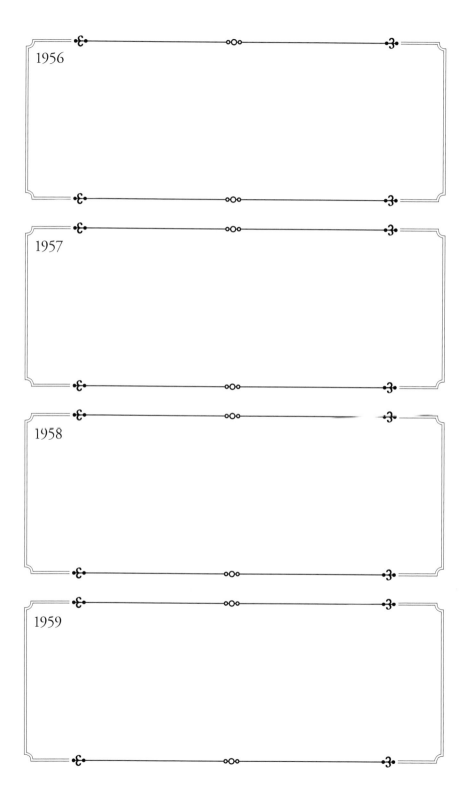

1956

1957

1958

1959

2000

2001

2002

2003

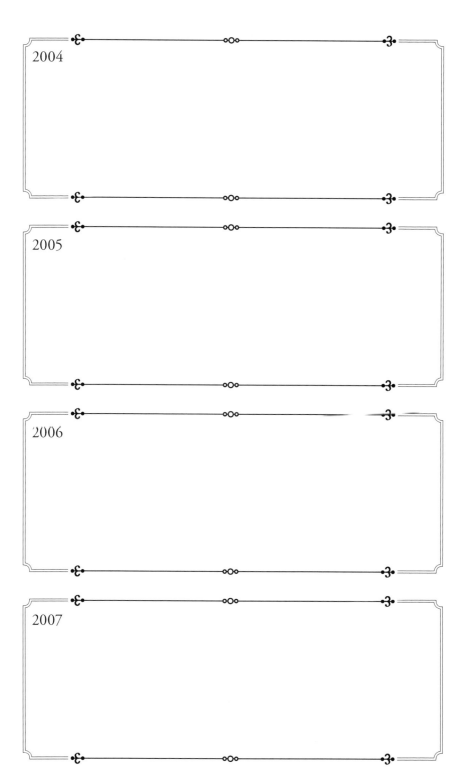

2004

2005

2006

2007

2008

2009

2010

2011

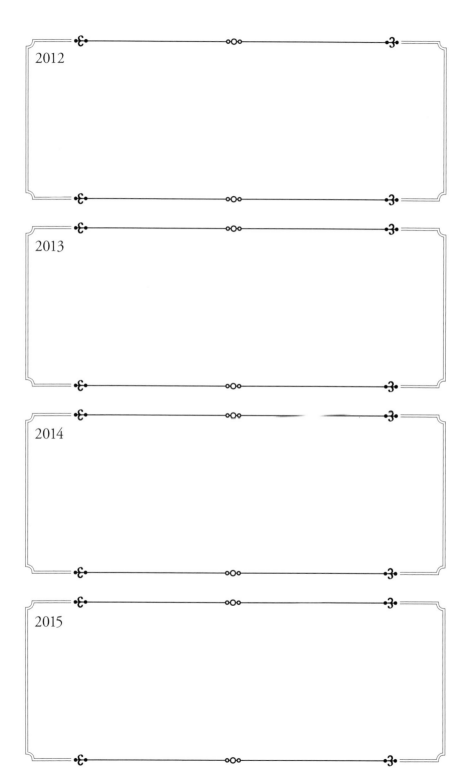

2012

2013

2014

2015

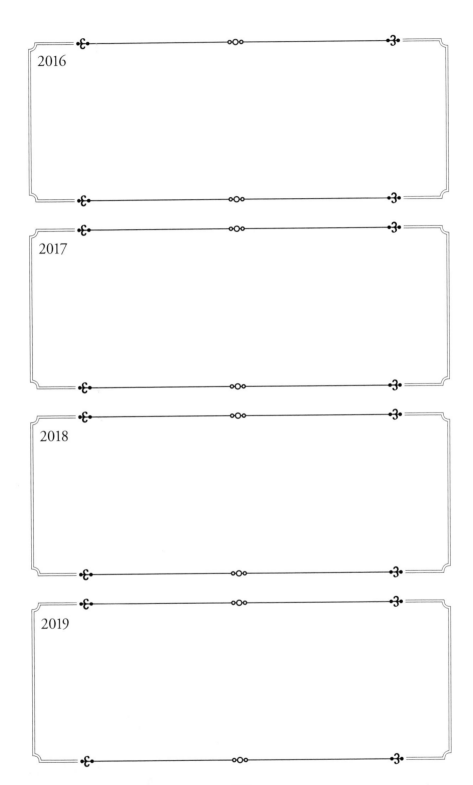

2016

2017

2018

2019

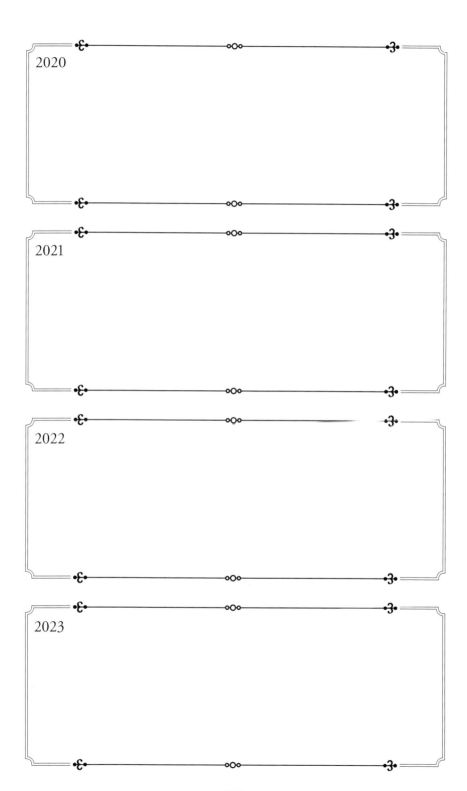

2020

2021

2022

2023

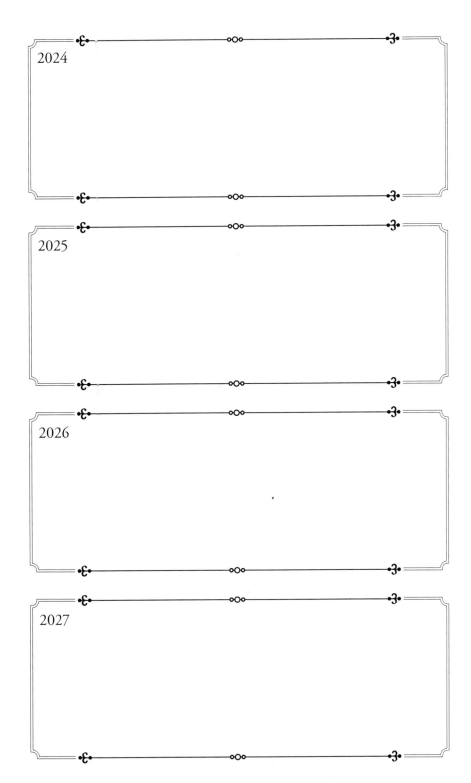

2024

2025

2026

2027

2028

2029

2030

2031

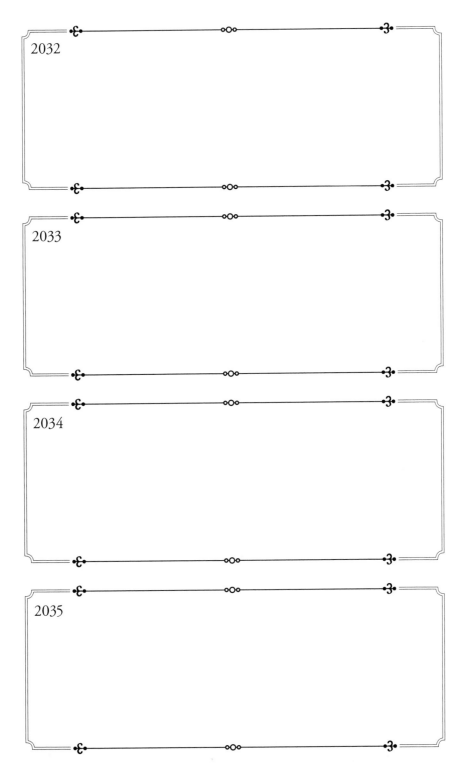

2032

2033

2034

2035

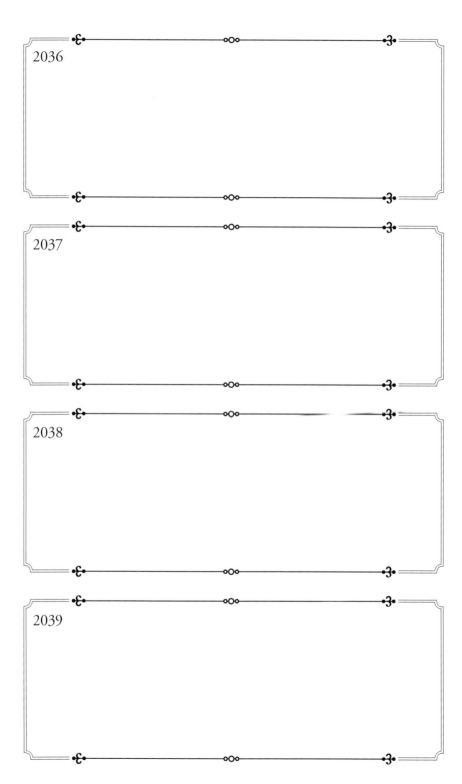

2036

2037

2038

2039

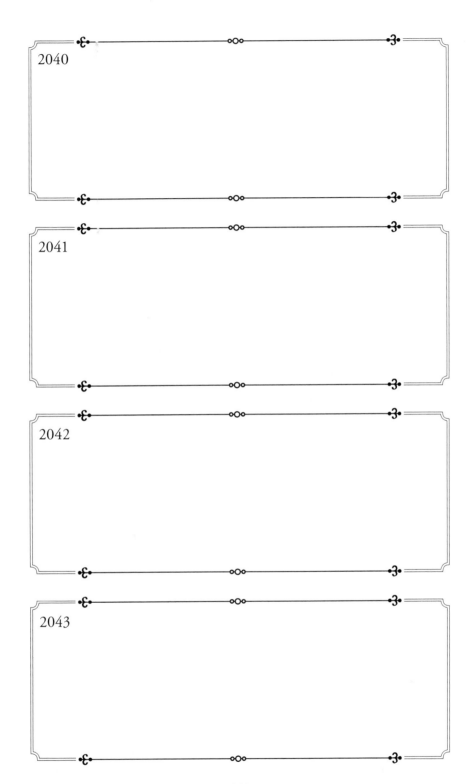

2040

2041

2042

2043

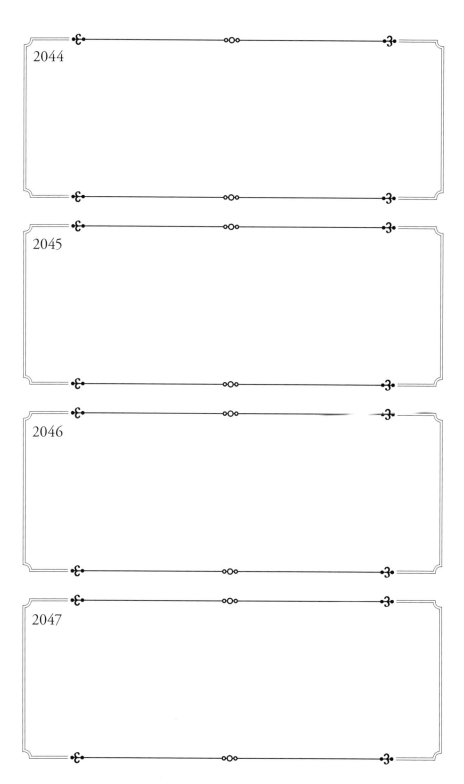

2044

2045

2046

2047

2048

2049

2050

2051

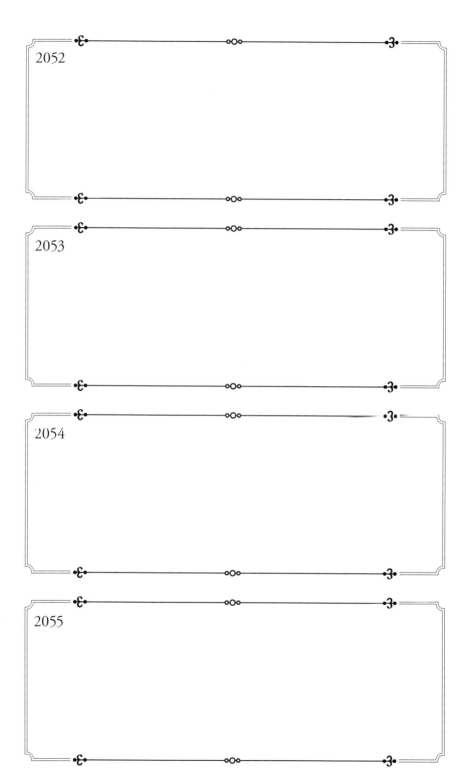

2052

2053

2054

2055

2056

2057

2058

2059

2100

2101

2102

2103

2104

2105

2106

2107

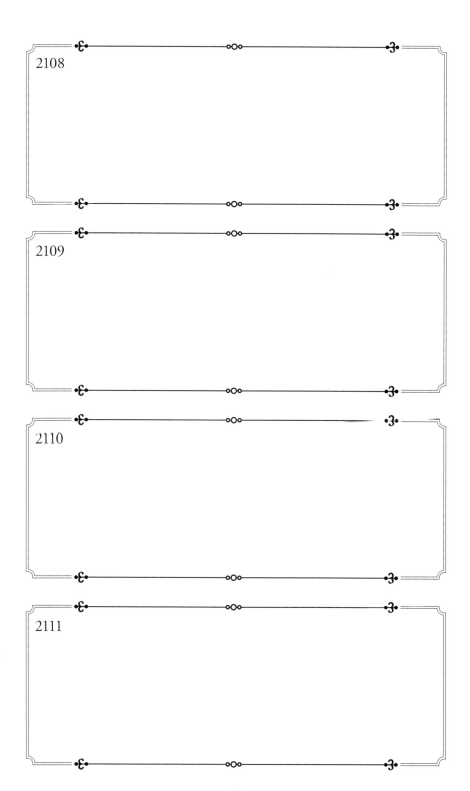

2108

2109

2110

2111

2112

2113

2114

2115

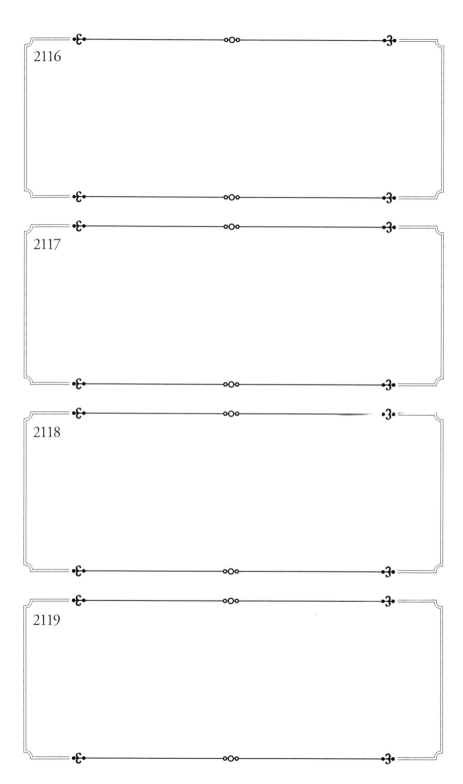

2116

2117

2118

2119

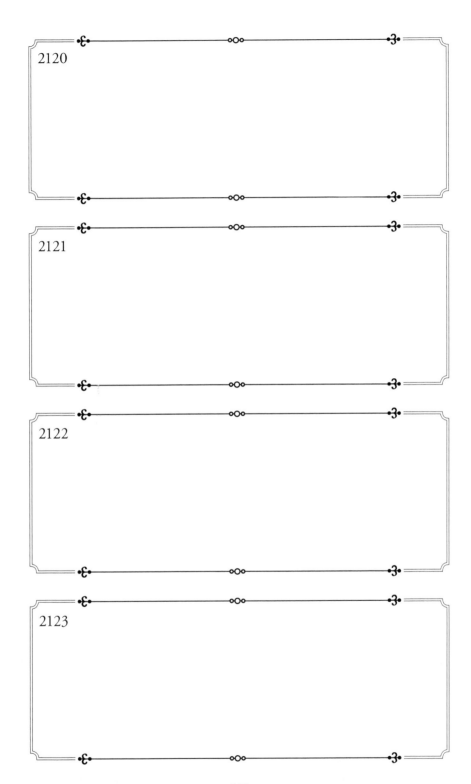

2120

2121

2122

2123

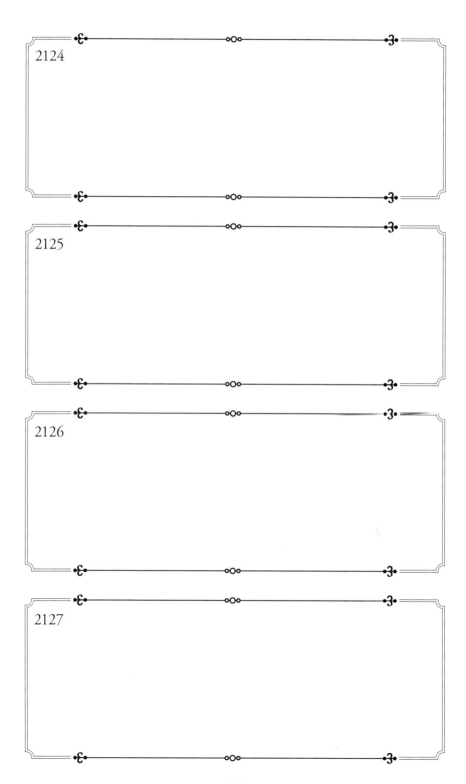

2124

2125

2126

2127

2128

2129

2130

2131

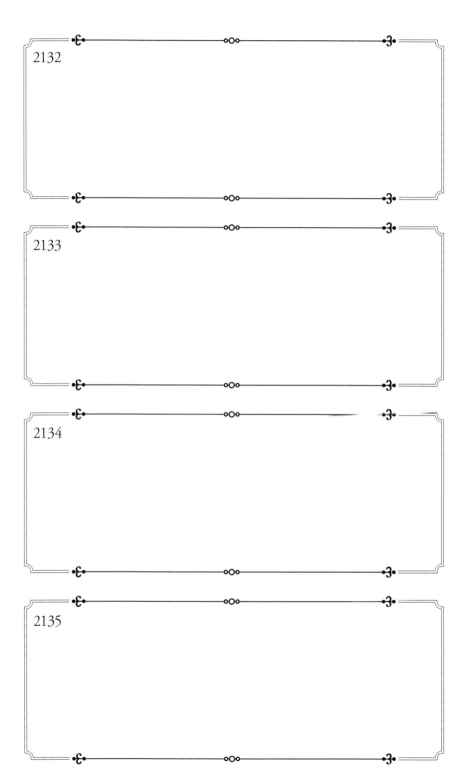

2132

2133

2134

2135

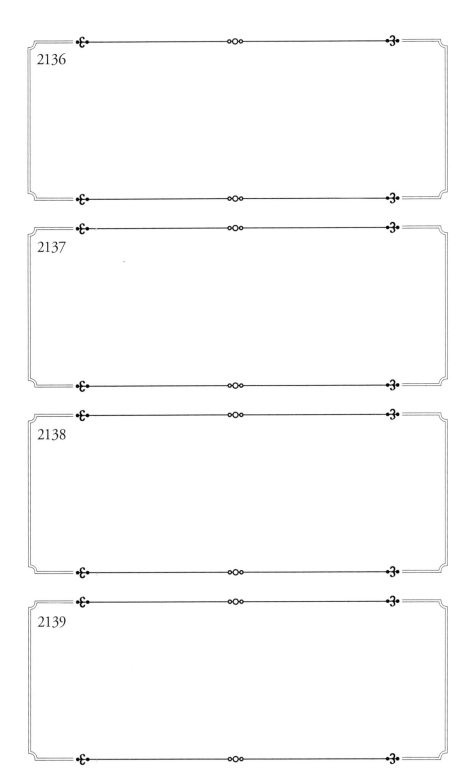

2136

2137

2138

2139

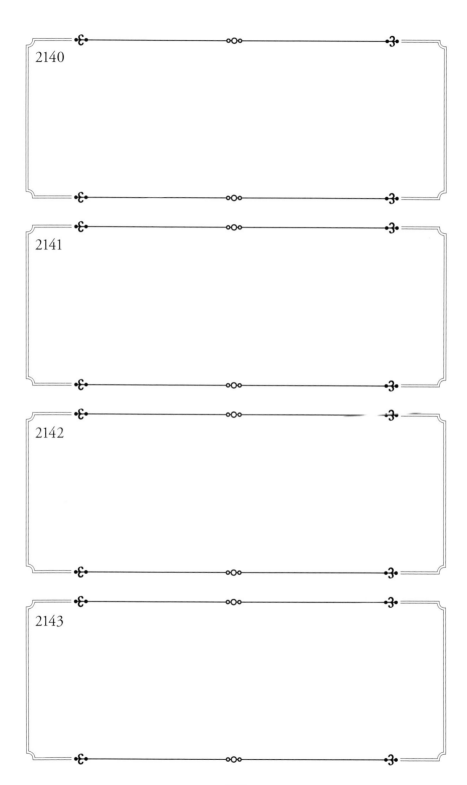

2140

2141

2142

2143

2144

2145

2146

2147

244

2148

2149

2150

2151

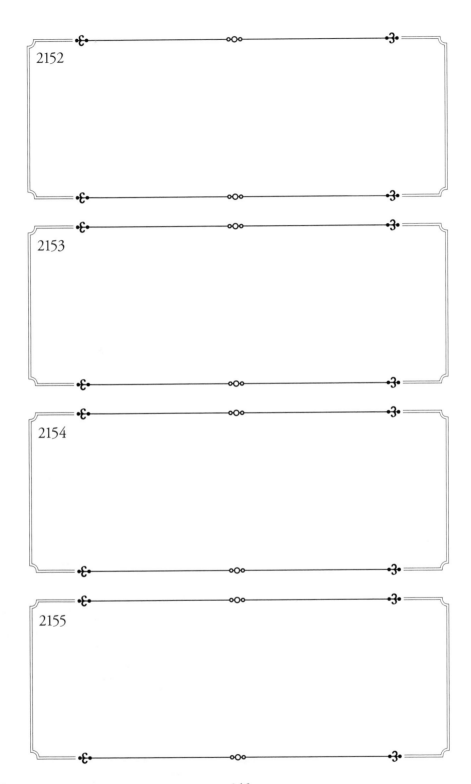

2152

2153

2154

2155

2156

2157

2158

2159

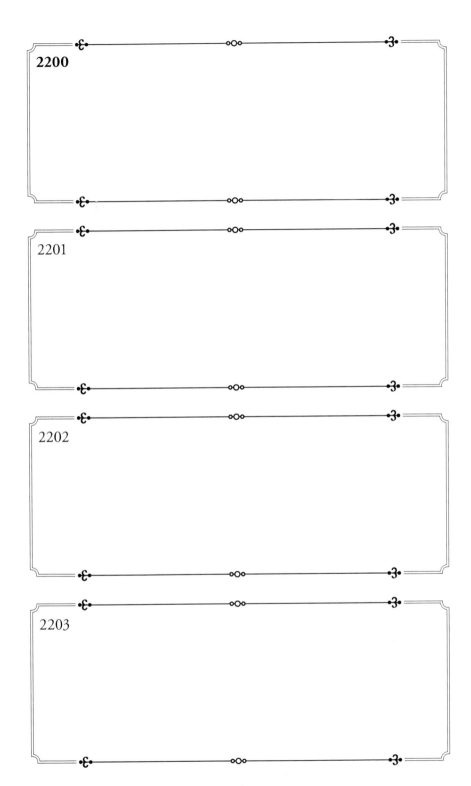

2200

2201

2202

2203

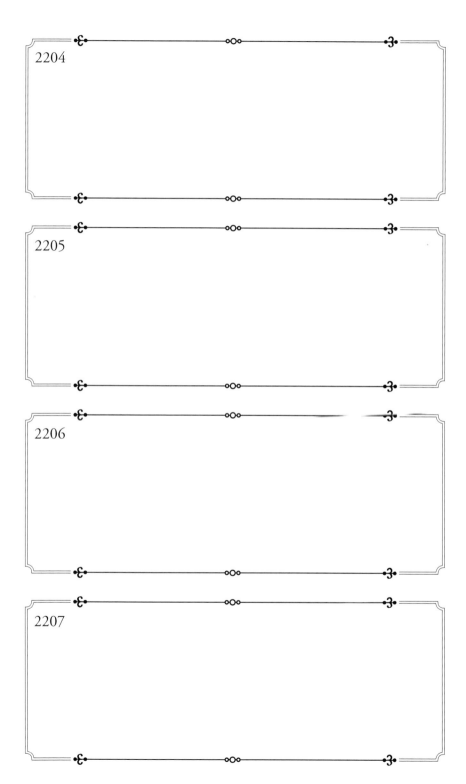

2204

2205

2206

2207

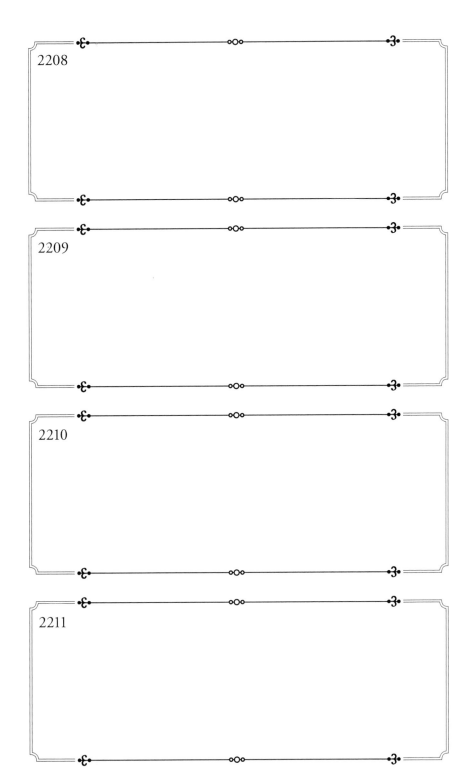

2208

2209

2210

2211

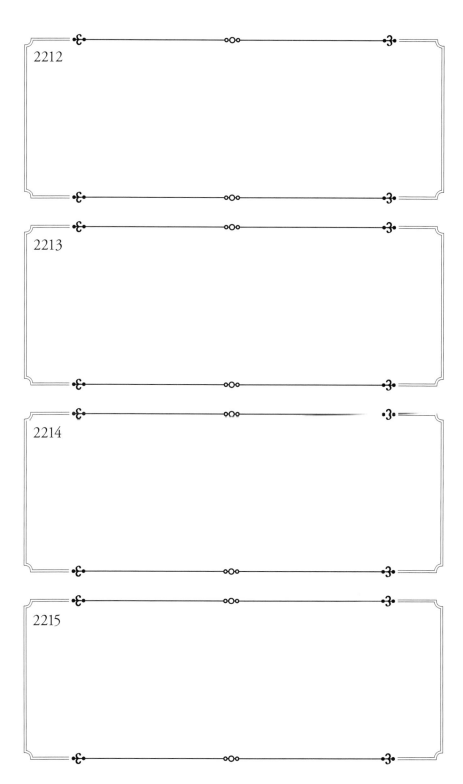

2212

2213

2214

2215

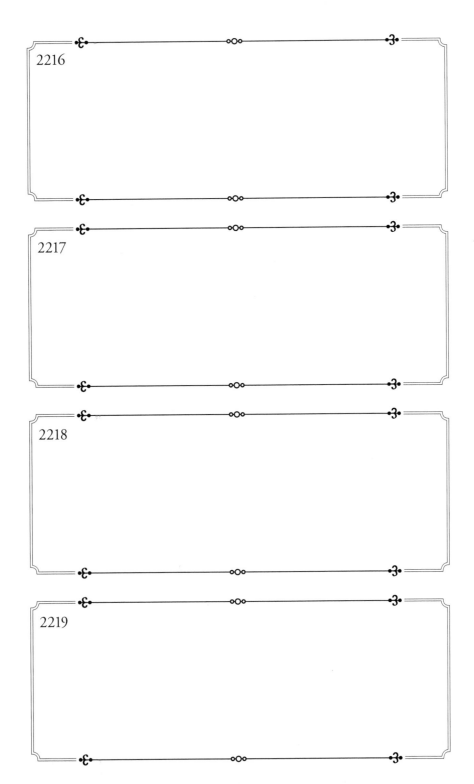

2216

2217

2218

2219

2220

2221

2222

2223

2224

2225

2226

2227

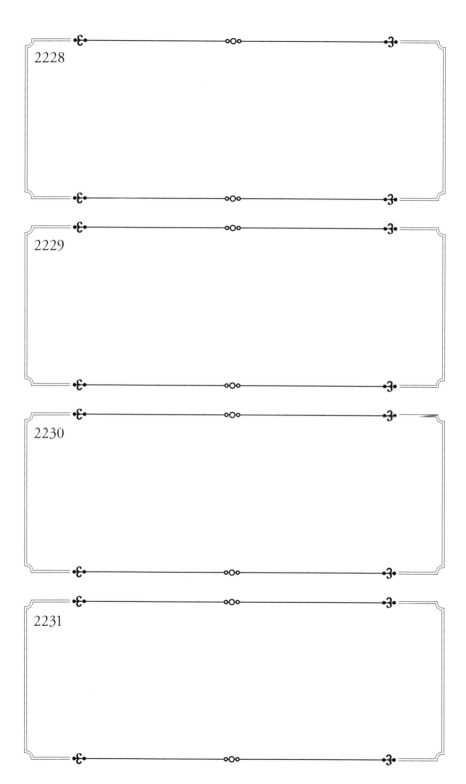

2228

2229

2230

2231

2232

2233

2234

2235

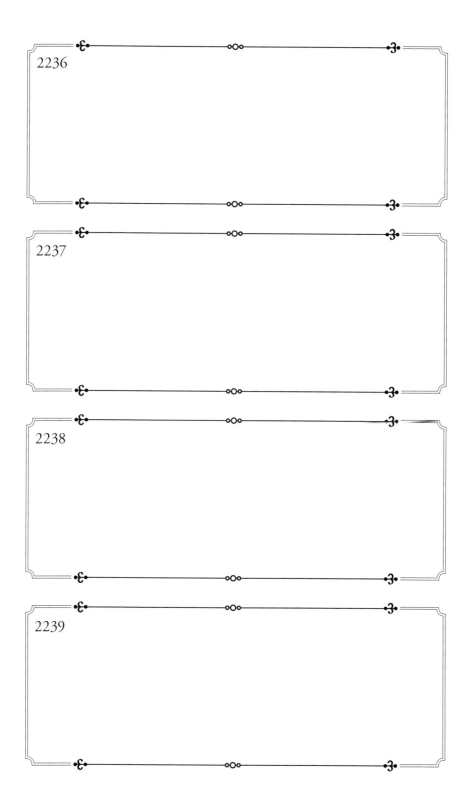

2236

2237

2238

2239

2240

2241

2242

2243

2244

2245

2246

2247

2248

2249

2250

2251

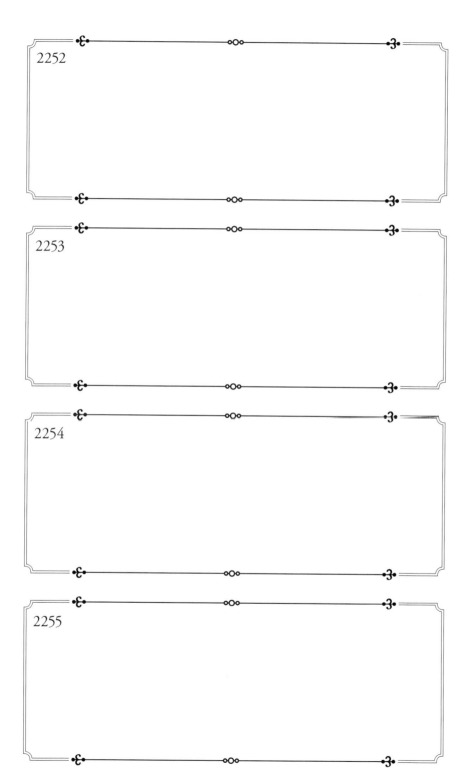

2252

2253

2254

2255

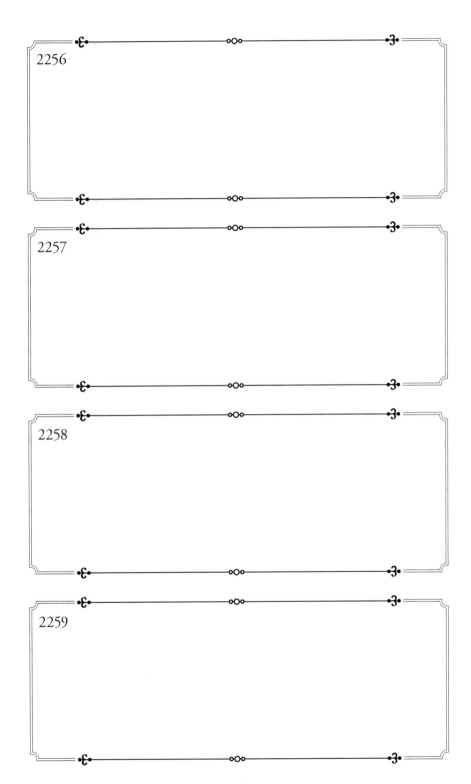

2256

2257

2258

2259

2300

2301

2302

2303

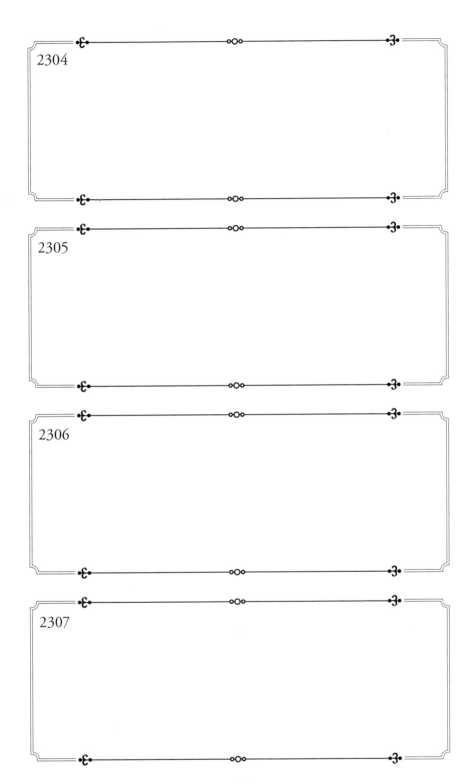

2304

2305

2306

2307

2308

2309

2310

2311

2312

2313

2314

2315

2316

2317

2318

2319

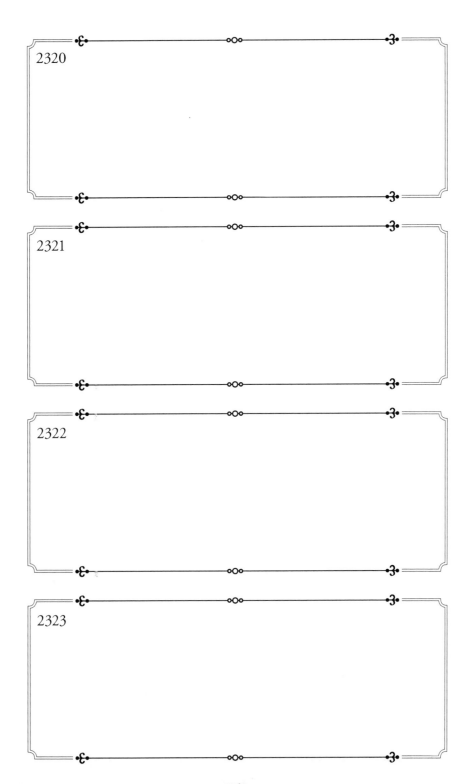

2320

2321

2322

2323

2324

2325

2326

2327

2328

2329

2330

2331

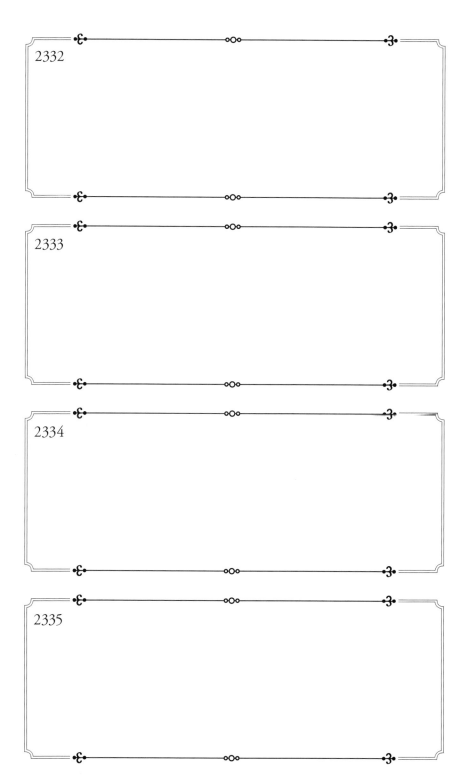

2332

2333

2334

2335

2336

2337

2338

2339

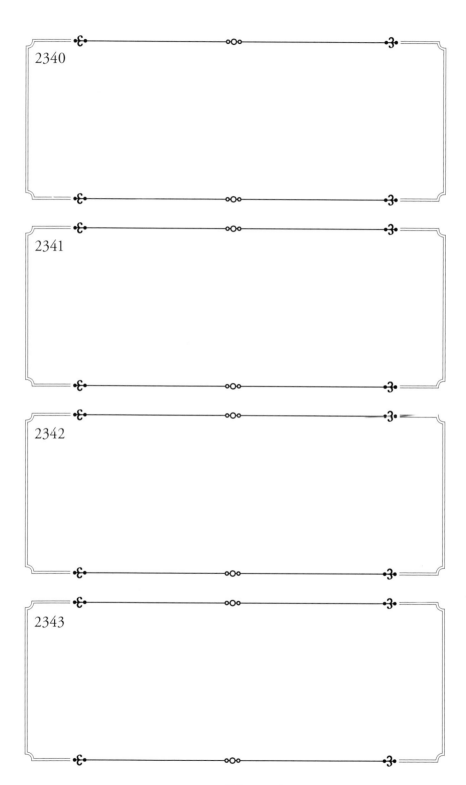

2340

2341

2342

2343

2344

2345

2346

2347

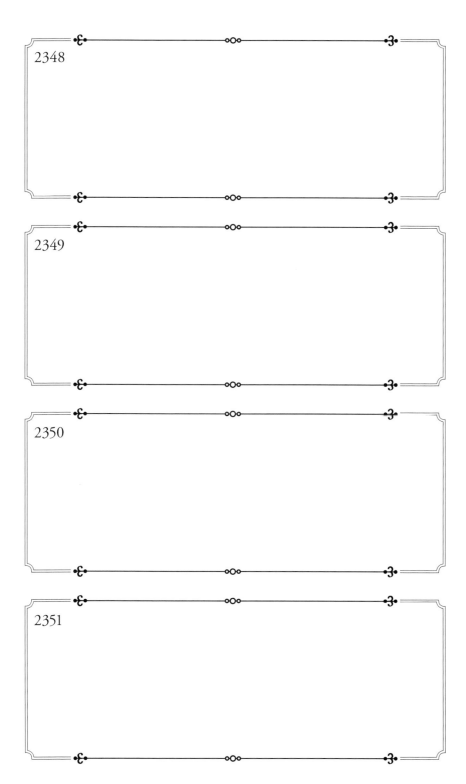

2348

2349

2350

2351

2352

2353

2354

2355

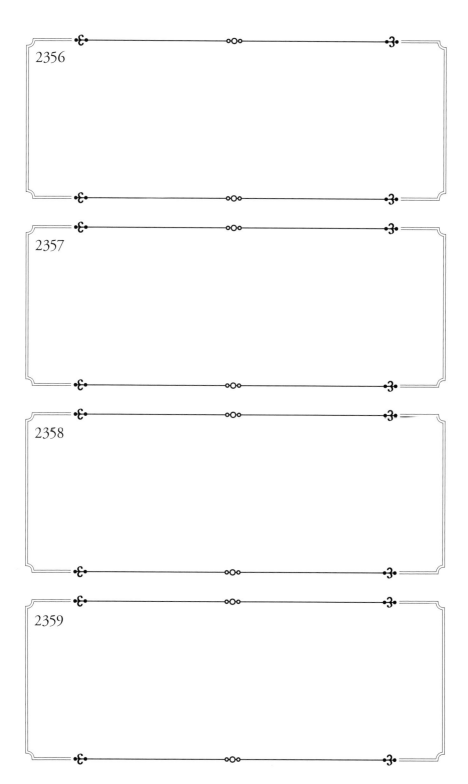

2356

2357

2358

2359

2400

2401

2402

2403

2404

2405

2406

2407

2408

2409

2410

2411

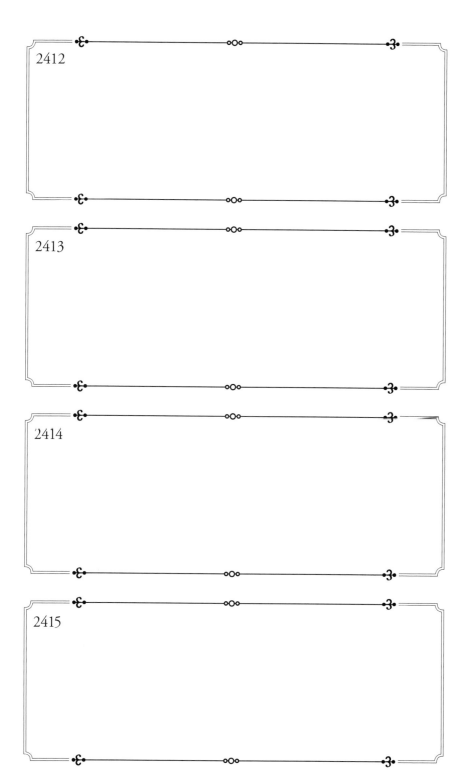

2412

2413

2414

2415

2416

2417

2418

2419

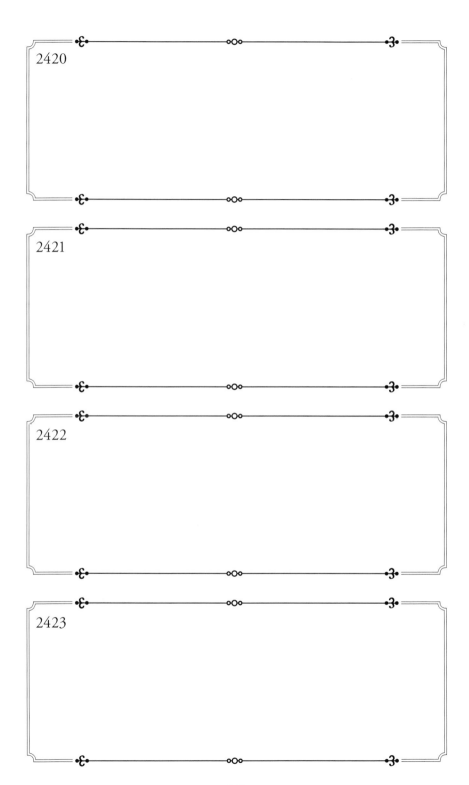

2420

2421

2422

2423

2424

2425

2426

2427

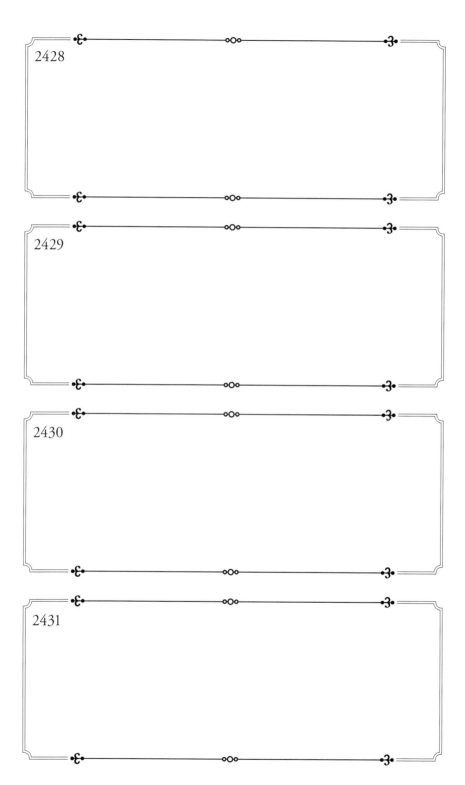

2428

2429

2430

2431

2432

2433

2434

2435

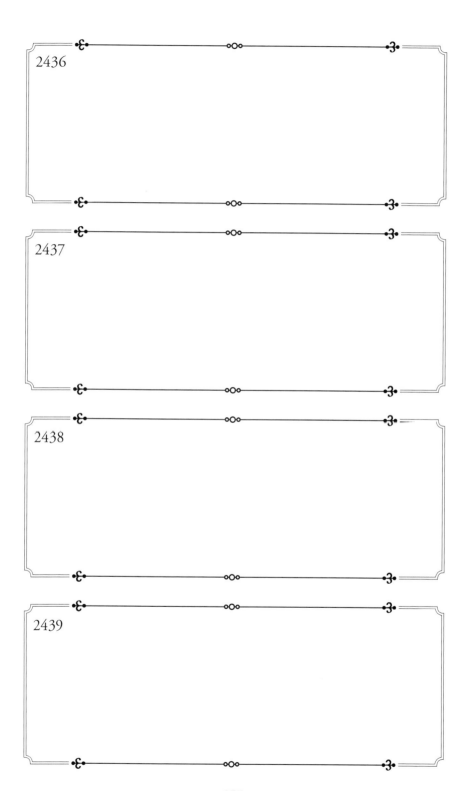

2436

2437

2438

2439

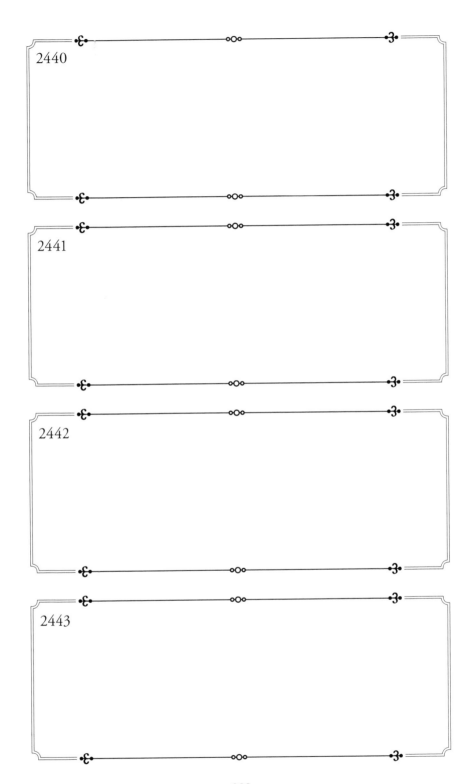

2440

2441

2442

2443

2444

2445

2446

2447

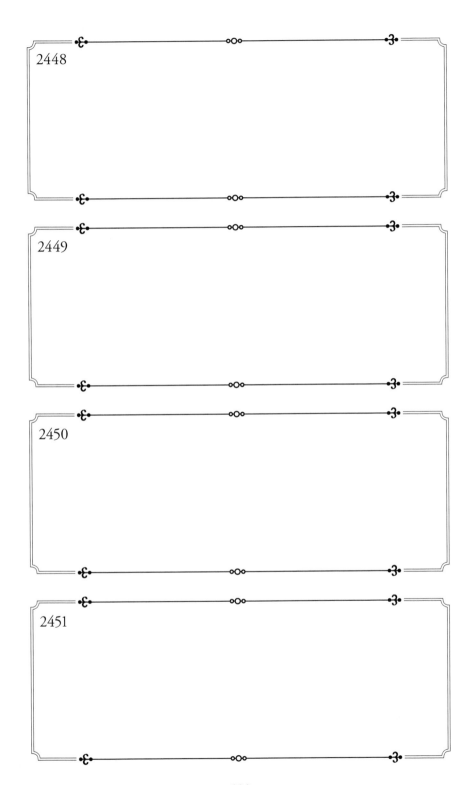

2448

2449

2450

2451

2452

2453

2454

2455

2456

2457

2458

2459

0100

0101

0102

0103

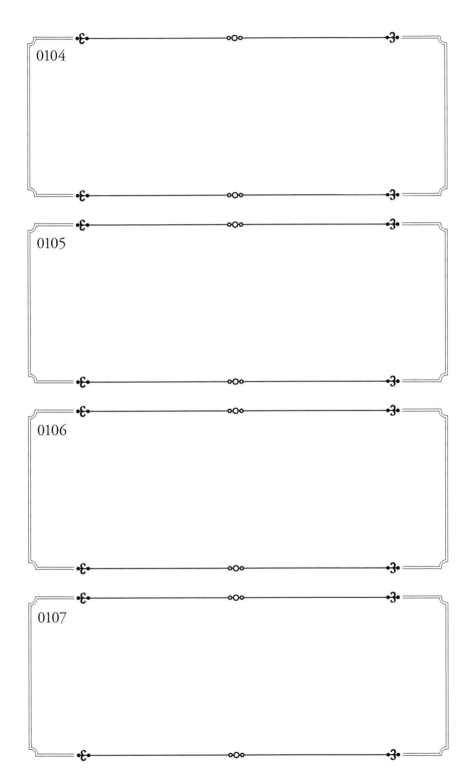

0104

0105

0106

0107

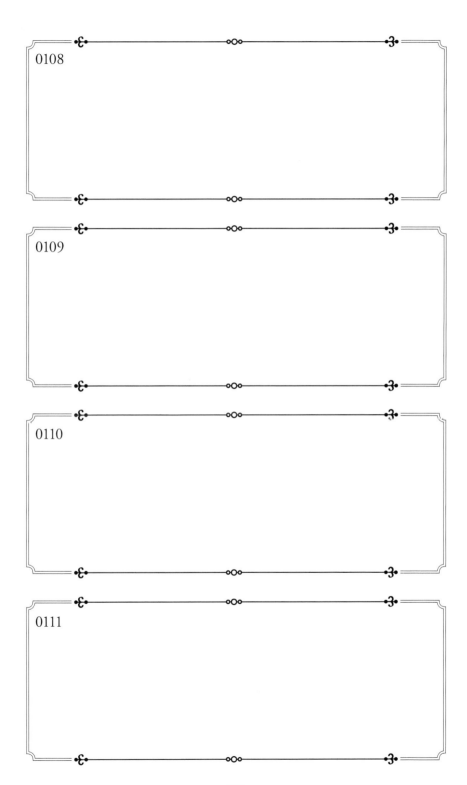

0108

0109

0110

0111

0112

0113

0114

0115

0116

0117

0118

0119

0120

0121

0122

0123

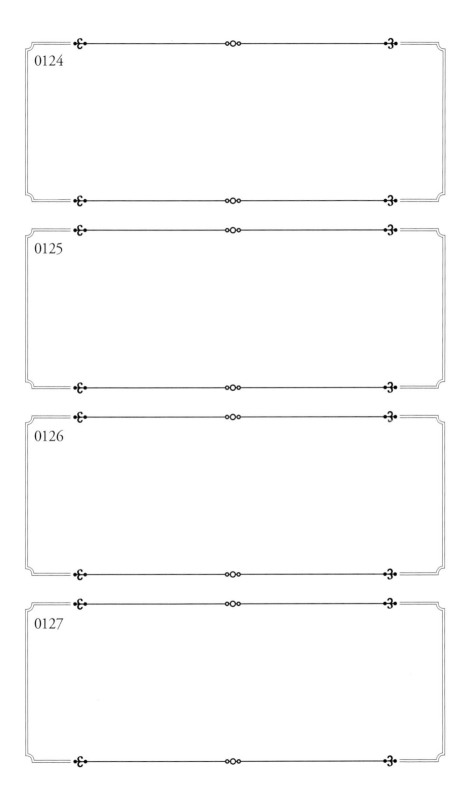

0124

0125

0126

0127

0128

0129

0130

0131

0132

0133

0134

0135

0136

0137

0138

0139

0140

0141

0142

0143

0144

0145

0146

0147

0148

0149

0150

0151

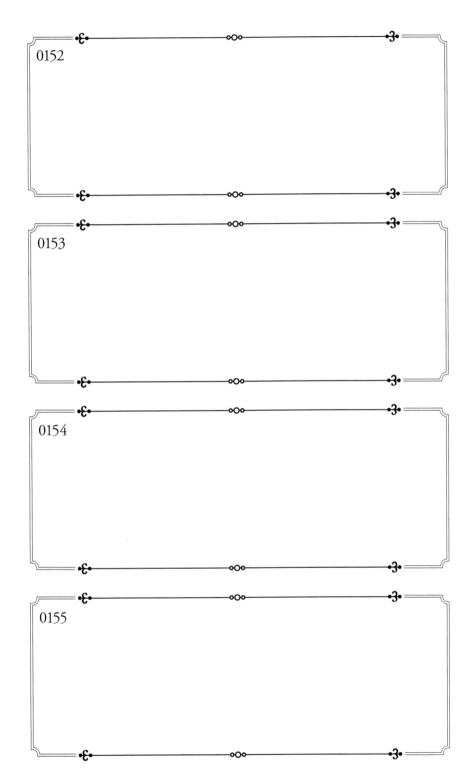

0152

0153

0154

0155

0156

0157

0158

0159

0200

0201

0202

0203

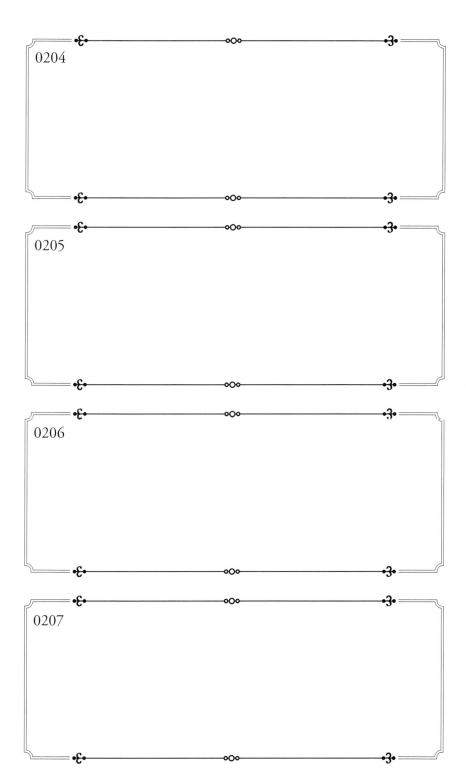

0204

0205

0206

0207

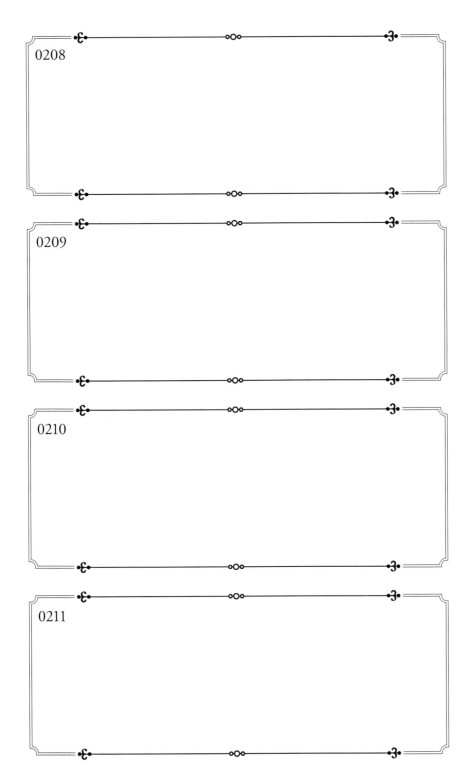

0208

0209

0210

0211

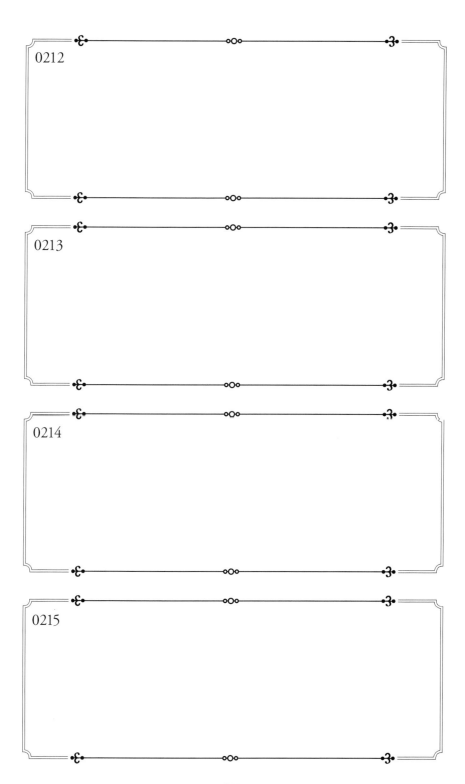

0212

0213

0214

0215

0216

0217

0218

0219

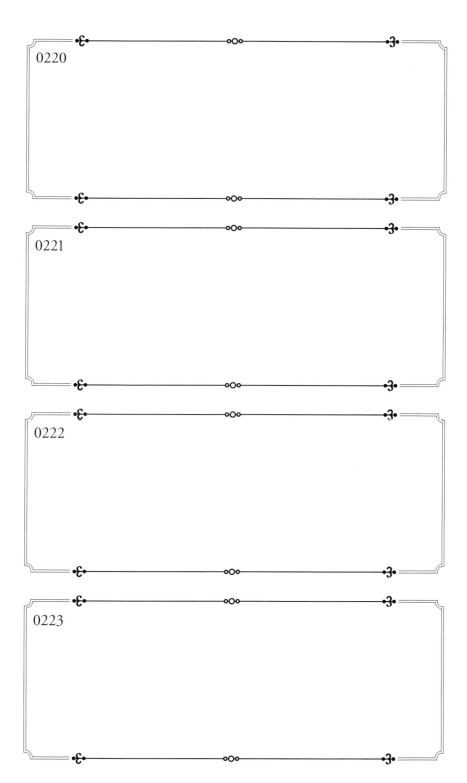

0220

0221

0222

0223

0224

0225

0226

0227

0228

0229

0230

0231

0232

0233

0234

0235

0236

0237

0238

0239

0240

0241

0242

0243

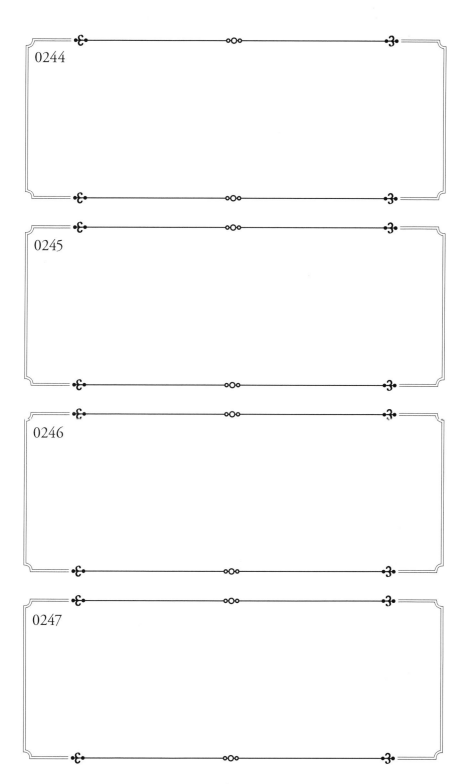

0244

0245

0246

0247

0248

0249

0250

0251

0252

0253

0254

0255

0256

0257

0258

0259

0300

0301

0302

0303

0304

0305

0306

0307

0308

0309

0310

0311

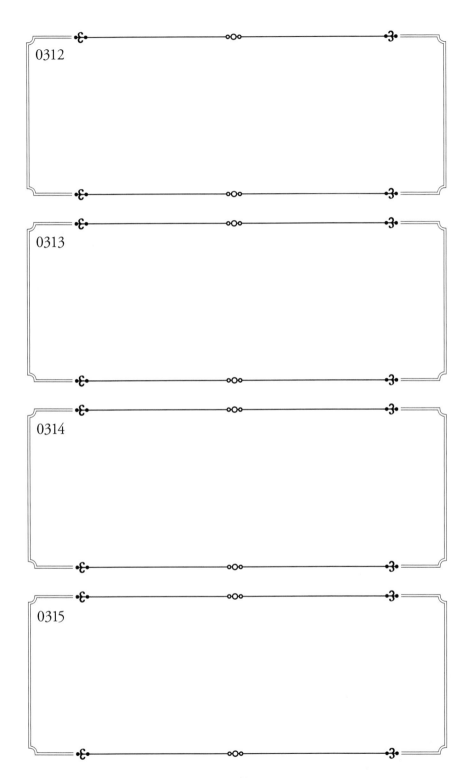

0312

0313

0314

0315

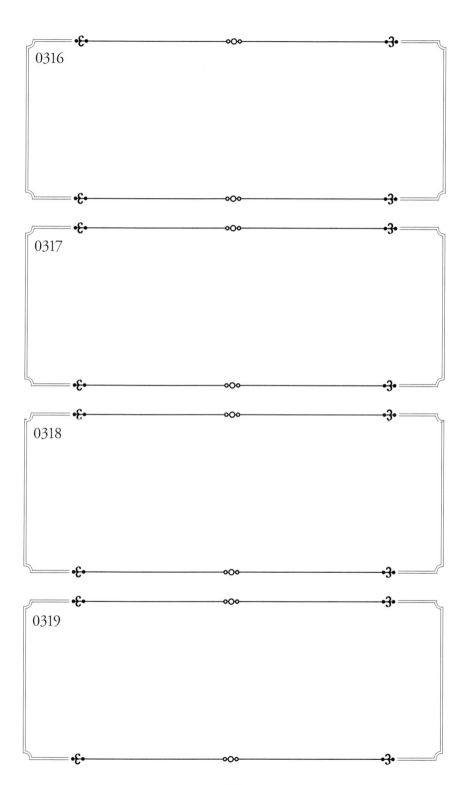

0316

0317

0318

0319

0320

0321

0322

0323

0324

0325

0326

0327

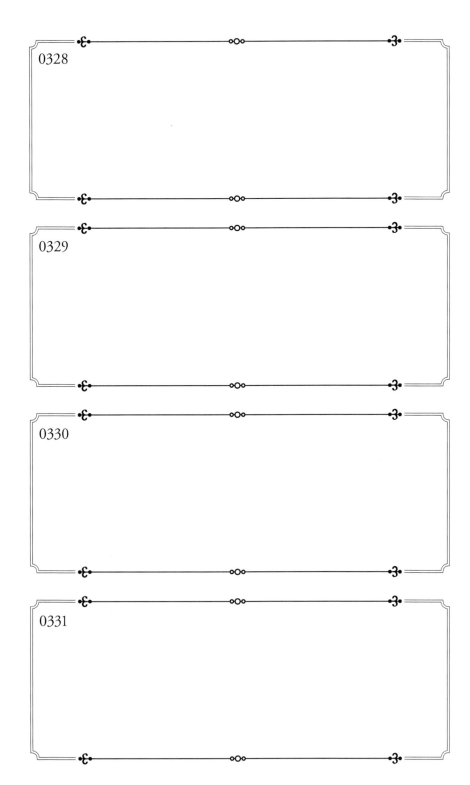

0328

0329

0330

0331

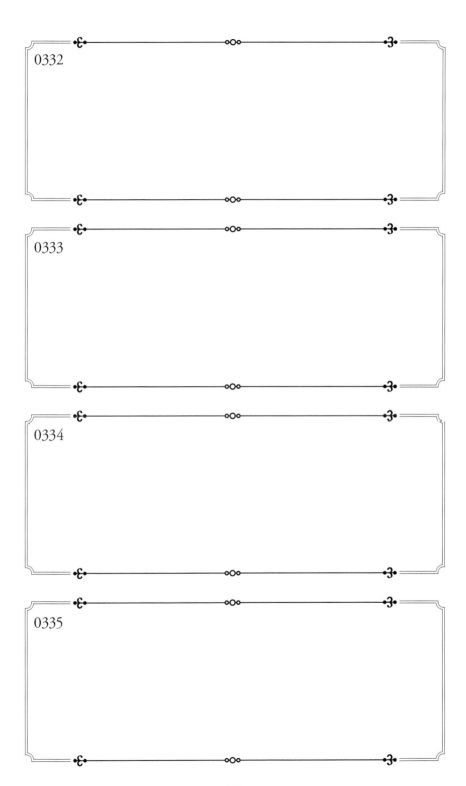

0332

0333

0334

0335

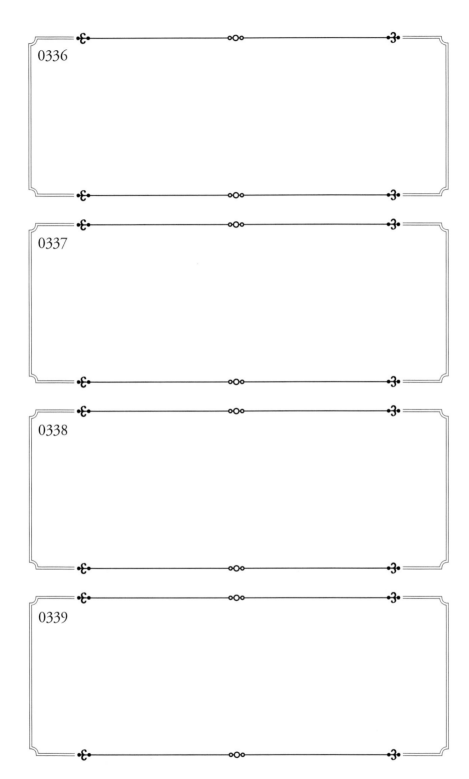

0336

0337

0338

0339

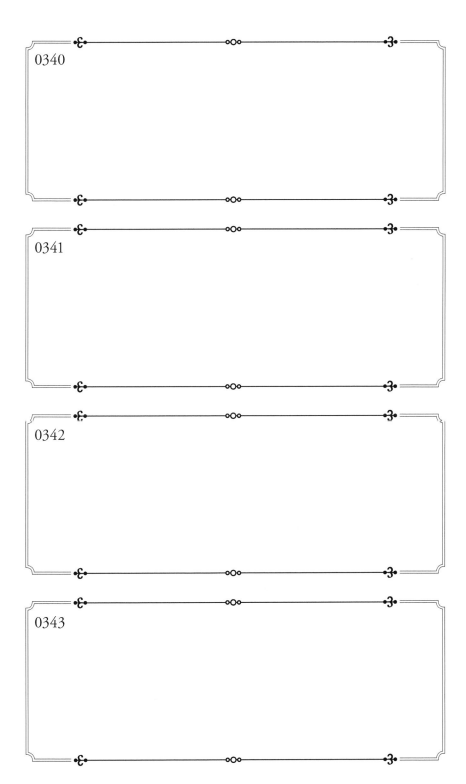

0340

0341

0342

0343

0344

0345

0346

0347

0348

0349

0350

0351

0352

0353

0354

0355

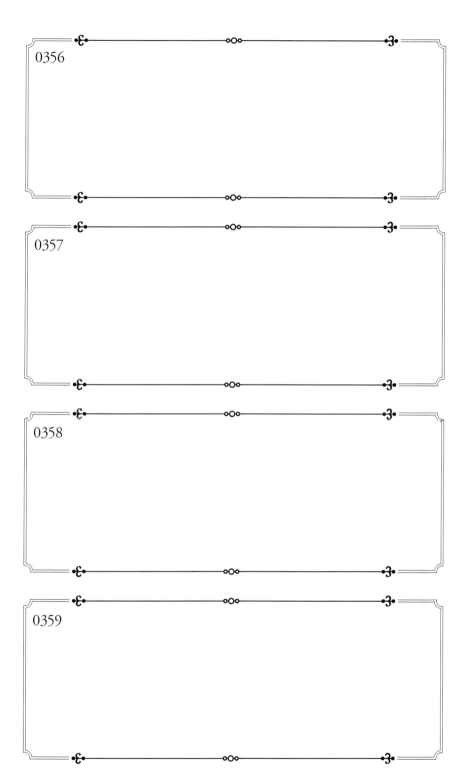

0356

0357

0358

0359

0400

0401

0402

0403

0404

0405

0406

0407

0408

0409

0410

0411

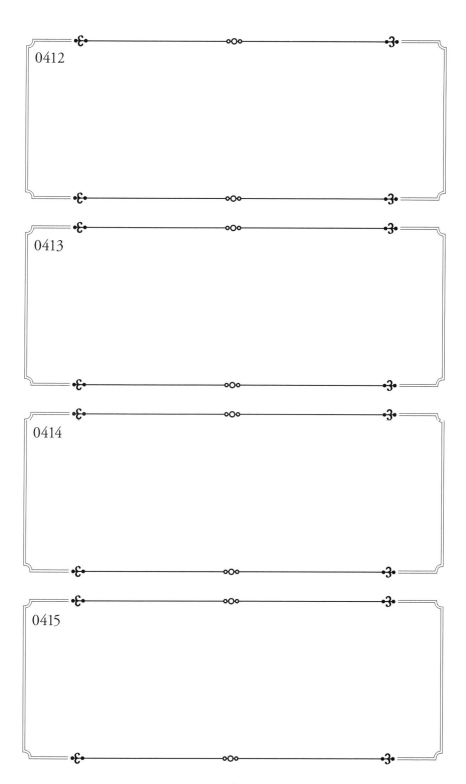

0412

0413

0414

0415

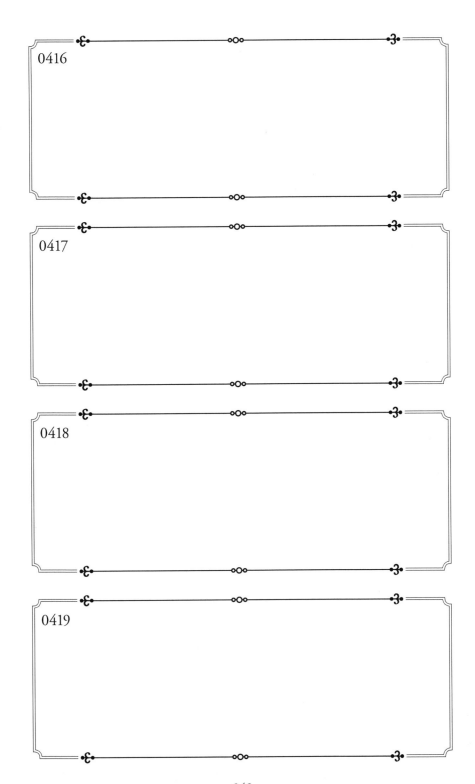

0416

0417

0418

0419

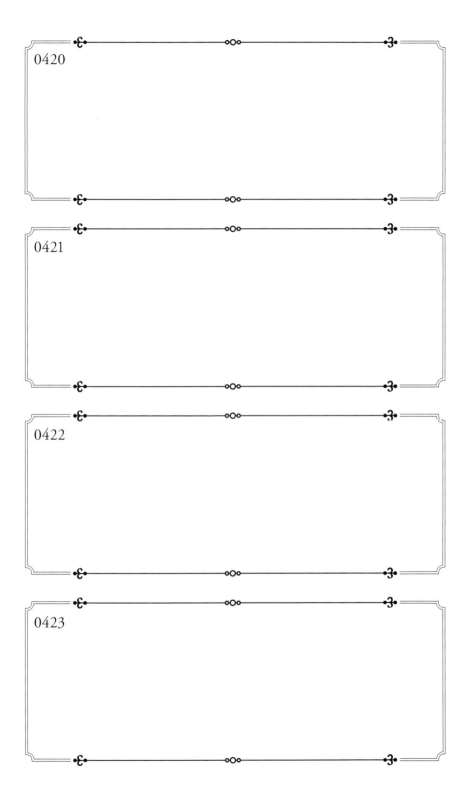

0420

0421

0422

0423

0424

0425

0426

0427

0428

0429

0430

0431

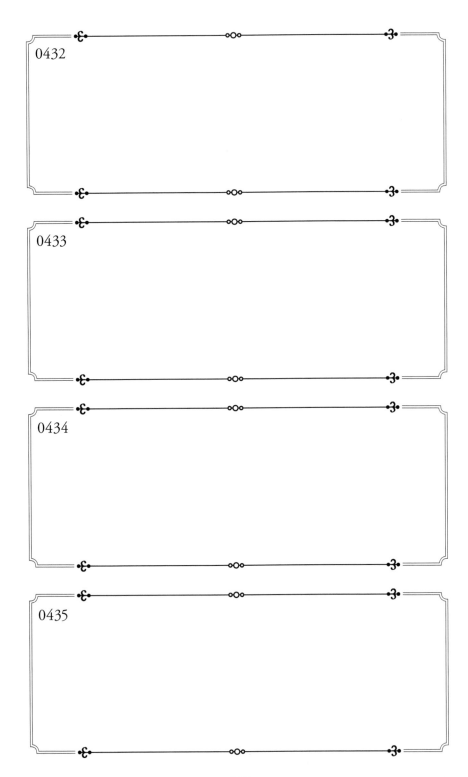

0432

0433

0434

0435

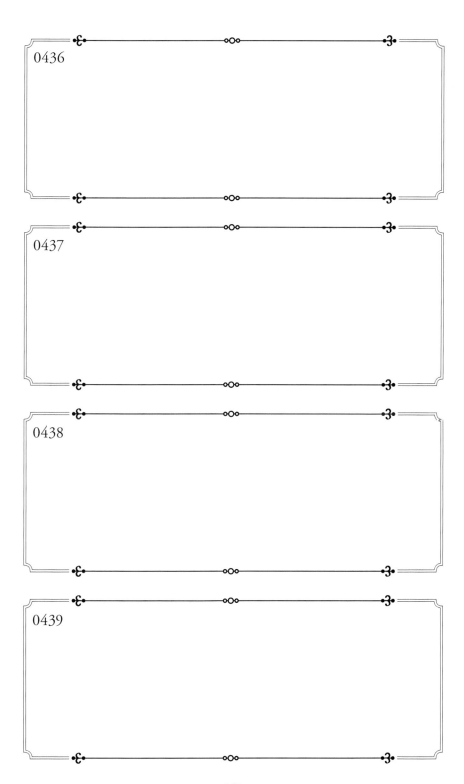

0436

0437

0438

0439

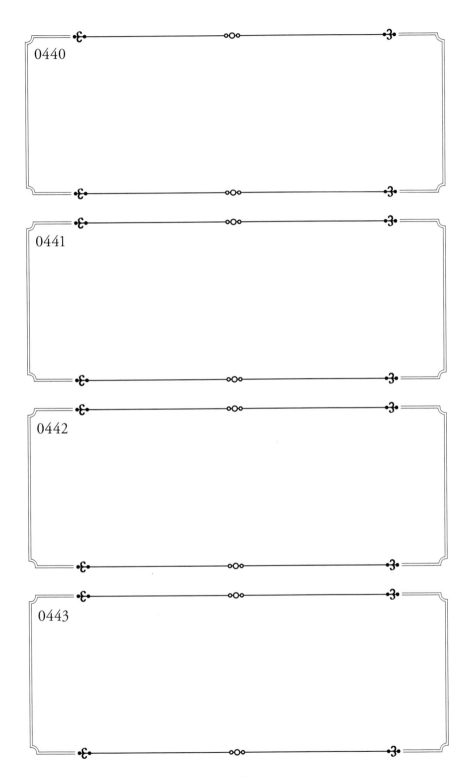

0440

0441

0442

0443

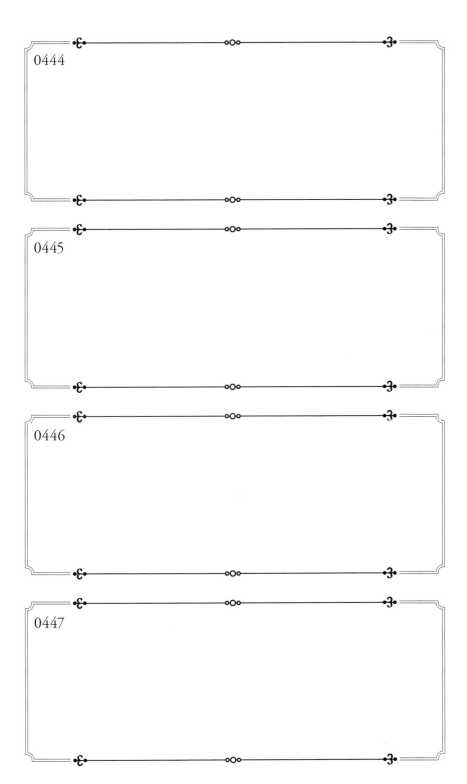

0444

0445

0446

0447

0448

0449

0450

0451

0452

0453

0454

0455

0456

0457

0458

0459

0500

0501

0502

0503

0504

0505

0506

0507

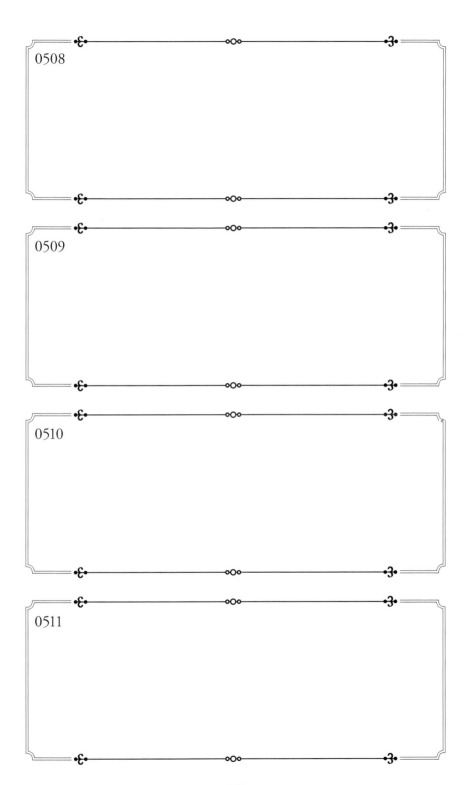

0508

0509

0510

0511

355

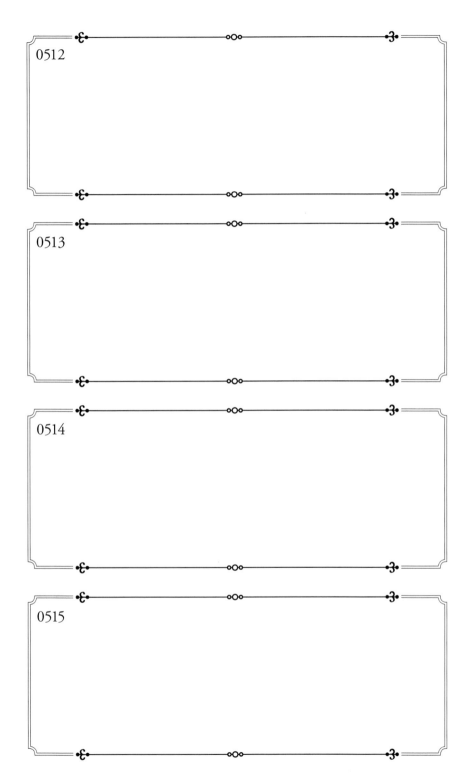

0512

0513

0514

0515

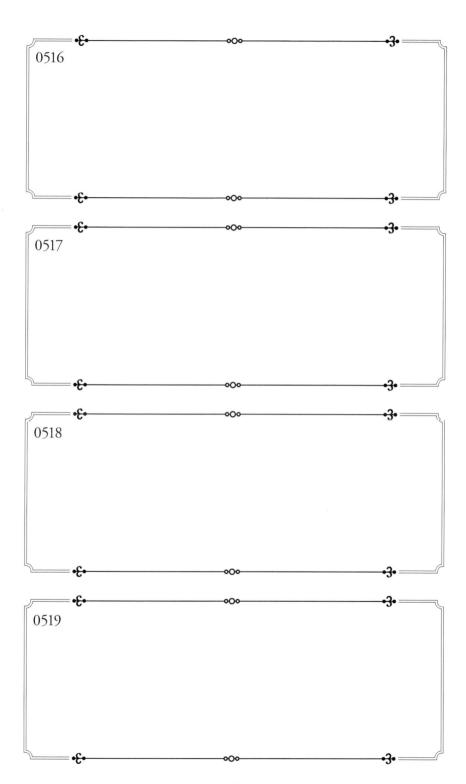

0516

0517

0518

0519

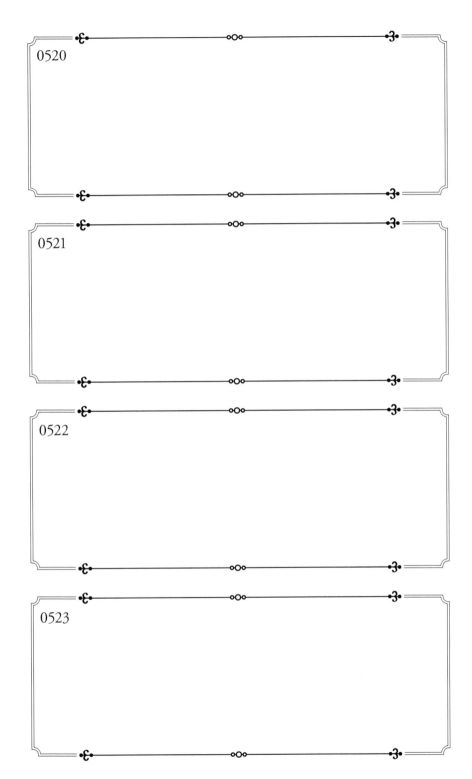

0520

0521

0522

0523

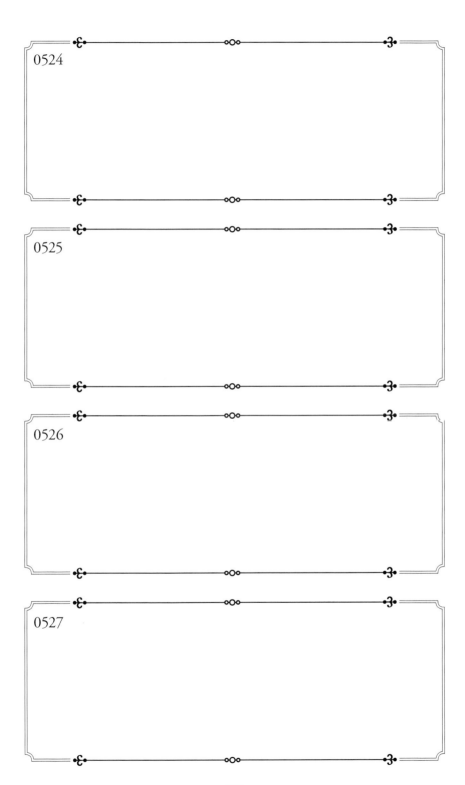

0524

0525

0526

0527

0528

0529

0530

0531

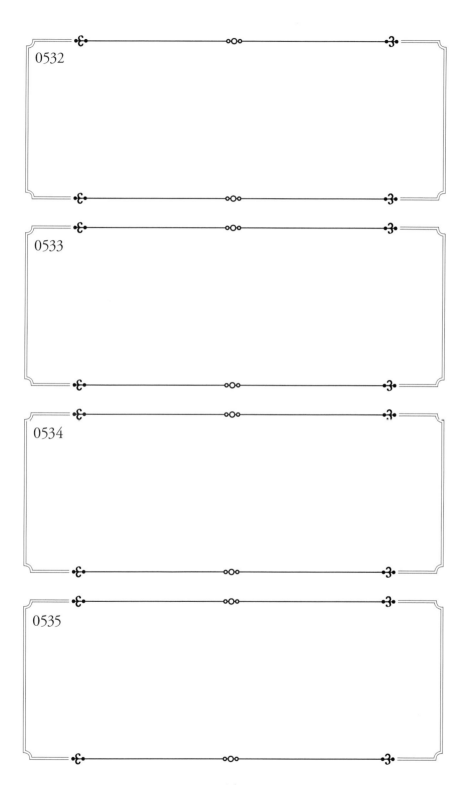

0532

0533

0534

0535

0536

0537

0538

0539

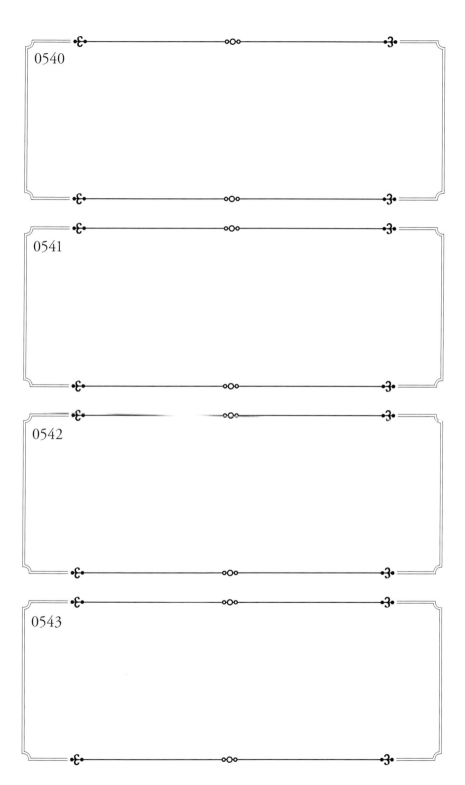

0540

0541

0542

0543

0544

0545

0546

0547

0548

0549

0550

0551

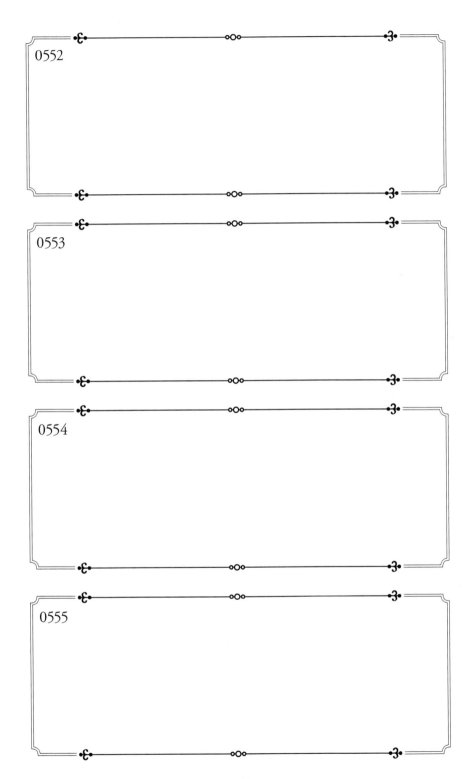

0552

0553

0554

0555

0556

0557

0558

0559

NOTES

Printed in the United States
By Bookmasters